─────Other Books by Leslie F. Brandt

Book of Christian Prayer

Bible Readings for Troubled Times

Bible Readings for the Retired

Meditations along the Journey of Faith

Meditations on a Loving God

Great God, Here I Am

Psalms/Now

Prophets/Now

Jesus/Now

Epistles/Now

God Is Here, Let's Celebrate!

Books by Leslie and Edith Brandt
Growing Together: Prayers for Married People

Two Minutes with God

Leslie F. Brandt

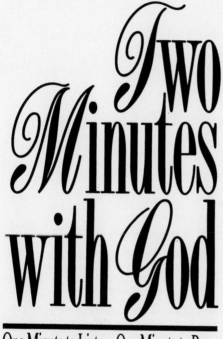

Two Minutes with God

One Minute to Listen, One Minute to Pray

AUGSBURG Publishing House
Minneapolis

TWO MINUTES WITH GOD
One Minute to Listen, One Minute to Pray

Library of Congress Cataloging-in-Publication Data

Brandt, Leslie F.
    Two minutes with God : one minute to listen, one minute to pray /
Leslie F. Brandt.
        p.   cm.
    ISBN 0-8066-2350-0
    1. Meditations. 2. Prayers. I. Title.
BV4832.2.B72   1988
242—dc19   88-6326
                                                                          CIP

Manufactured in the U.S.A.   APH 10-6724

        2   3   4   5   6   7   8   9   0   1   2   3   4   5   6   7   8   9

Preface

The older I become, the shorter become my messages—spoken or written. I am now down to *Two Minutes with God*. I do not, however, want any of my readers to think I am in favor of "religion-on-the-run." Our times truly are in God's hands, and God's continual presence with us along the journey of faith is essential to our spiritual health and well-being.

Yet there are those days when two minutes may be all that we have to catch our breath and determine our direction on our course before us. And those two minutes may turn out to be the most important two minutes of the day—one minute to listen, one minute to pray.

For the first minute, read the Bible selection and the meditation, listening to what God tells you through those words. Use the second minute to pray the prayer on the opposite page, adding your own words if you wish.

I hope these short messages and prayers may comfort or encourage, provoke or challenge you along your faith journey. God help each one of us to recognize and remember that we are his children and servants, and that means every day of every week, whatever our activities and avocations.

May we be continually assured of God's love and concern for each of us—whatever the 1,440 minutes of each day may bring forth.

1————Time Out

*M*ark 6:30-32 "Come with me by your-
selves to a quiet place and get some rest" (v. 31).

Thomas Merton wrote: "Of all the violence in our
world, perhaps the greatest violence is that of our busy
lives." One of the reasons for "burn-out" in the lives of
so many who spend most of the days of each week in
the fast lane of this life's activities is the neglect of or the
inability to take time-outs. The wise coach knows when
it becomes necessary to call a time-out, especially when
the game appears to be tense and high-pitched. Whether
your activity is "for the work of the Lord" or is fully
occupied with secular functions, time-outs are very important for both the physical and spiritual aspect of your
being.

This is not merely a suggestion that you "take time
to be holy" as an old hymn enjoins. "My times are in
[God's] hands," claimed the psalmist. You are also continually in God's hands, and you are never absolved
from your commission as the servant and minister of
God's purposes. Nor are two-minute time-outs to listen
and to speak with God, as this little volume indicates,
sufficient for Christian growth and service. There must
be, however, "rest stops" along the fast lane that are
utilized and dedicated to worship. They would provide
times for spiritual relaxation, renewal, and comfort as
well as challenge.

Take time-outs for meditation and prayer along the
journey of faith. They will calm the spirit and clear the
vision, and they will help you to stay on course when
the way is dark and lonely.

Prayer for the Day

There are those days, dear Lord,
   when nothing seems to work—
   when I could just as well have stayed in bed.
All my hustling and bustling appears to be in vain,
   and it seems that I get tripped up or beaten down
   regardless of what I attempt to do.
There are too many mouths to feed, bills to pay.
People expect too much of me;
   I can't be what people want me to be
   or do everything I am supposed to do.
No matter how hard I try,
   I just can't run fast enough or work hard enough
   to make ends meet or hold everything together.
My relationship to you may be in jeopardy, O God.
I need to take a time-out and lean on your grace
   to repair the spiritual damage that this
   fast-lane living may do to our relationship.
I sincerely want to serve you, Lord.
Help me to be aware that even while I thrash
   about in frantic activity,
   I need often the serenity of quietly
   waiting upon you for mending and refilling.
May my days include ample time-outs
   to relate and commune with you.

2———God's Child and Servant Forever

1 Corinthians 1:26-31   "Think of what you were when you were called" (v. 26).

Perhaps you are not particularly wise—at least according to worldly standards. You probably have no power over the lives of others—or even when it comes to managing your own life. You may not have inherited any nobility, though your ancestors were rugged, noble people. It is possible that you do not possess the charisma that attracts followers or initiates fan clubs.

The good news is that this, according to Paul, may serve to make you eligible for servanthood in the kingdom of God. While God may very well use and speak through the gifted personalities about you—the powerful and influential, the bright and talented people who attract the spotlights while they occupy the great pulpits or stages of the world—history bears witness that God has more often revealed his love and purposes through men and women who were rejected, despised, imprisoned, even martyred by the communities in which they lived.

Whatever the world thinks about you, even if few people ever think about you at all, God chose you, however weak or foolish or failure-fraught you think yourself to be. God has, through Christ, set you free from sin, even from your hesitant feelings about yourself, to be his child and servant forever.

Prayer for the Day

I thank you, O Lord,
　　that you love and accept me as I am,
　　and not for what I might accomplish today.
Help me to accept myself as you accept me,
　　to face this day's problems and challenges
　　as your child and servant.
It is not so important that I be successful,
　　but that I be faithful,
　　that I belong to you,
　　that I represent and glorify you.
It is important, O God,
　　that I allow you to have your way
　　in and through me.
So be it, Lord.

3——Be What You Are

*M*atthew 6:25-34 "Look at the birds of the air. . . . See the lilies of the field . . ." (vv. 26, 28).

Is it possible that you may try too hard to be what you ought to be, or worry too much about doing what God may want you to do? What about the lilies of the field, the birds of the air—the sea, the sky, the sun and stars and moon? All these things simply *are*, and yet how wonderfully and beautifully they minister to the inhabitants of this planet. Christians hear a great deal about what they ought to be as disciples of Christ. They are challenged constantly—by God's Word as well as the preachers who proclaim it—to be more loving, more giving, more compassionate. Or they ought to pray more, study more, and work harder to carry out their Lord's objectives. "Dear friends, now we *are* children of God," writes John (1 John 3:2), "and what we will be has not yet been made known." Is your faith large enough to settle for what you are and to forego the nagging urge to be somebody or something else?

Christians must constantly stand with God in judgment over the sins, the self-centeredness, the fractures, and distortions of their inner nature. They must also, without anxious striving or worrisome struggling, be themselves as God created them and then redeemed them to be. "Let go and let God" may be an overused cliché, but it refers to the importance of ceasing your attempts to focus on what some admired personage appears to be, or what others expect you to be, and to concentrate on God who accepts and loves you as you are.

Prayer for the Day

Gracious Father, help me to be what I am,
to grow and bloom where I am planted,
to accept myself as a part of that vineyard
which bears fruit for you;
that I, by your grace, may touch the lives of
sad and lonely people about me
with your healing love.
Forgive me, my God, for aspiring and reaching
for those things never meant for me;
for conscious or unconscious efforts to be top-gun
or king-of-the-hill in my arena of service,
for competing for a position at the head table
rather than accepting my role as servant to others.
I praise you, O God, for creating and redeeming
me to be your child,
and for the joy and satisfaction of knowing
that I am significant to you,
despite the judgments and opinions
of my peers about me.

4———Keep on Loving

*P*hilippians 1:3-11   "And this is my prayer: that your love may abound more and more in knowledge and depth of insight" (v. 9).

Paul the apostle prayed that these Christians may be "filled with the fruit of righteousness that comes through Jesus Christ." His charge to them, and it is passed on to you, is that they—and you—keep on loving, loving God and loving one another. You need, in these difficult days, not only the everflowing grace of God which comes to you through the Spirit by way of the Word and the Lord's Supper, but the strength and encouragement that come through loving relationships with one another.

You can be as confident as Paul that God, who adopted you as his child and gifted you with the Holy Spirit, will finish this great thing he began in you and will "carry it on to completion until the day of Christ Jesus." Whatever the difficulties this day and this life hold for you, you are enjoined and encouraged to keep on loving. Whether or not others love you in return, by the grace of God, you can keep on loving—your family, friends, adversaries, especially your fellow laborers within the kingdom of God. This is God's role for you in your arena of this world today.

As you think through the experiences of your life, notice the many times you have loved someone: your parents, brothers and sisters, other family members, friends, a husband or wife, your own children or other children. Each time you love, you grow in your ability to love. God help you to keep on loving!

Prayer for the Day

O God, before I can be a disciple of Jesus Christ
and a servant to your children about me,
I must learn how to love.
Teach me, Lord, how to love your children,
whatever their race or creed or station in life,
to love them even as you love me and all
your other creatures.
It is my self-centeredness, my self-idolatry,
that prevents your love from flowing through me
to the lonely, unloved, deprived, and oppressed
people in my path.
May your great, eternal love so flood my life, that,
not only will my self-serving be forgiven,
but that it might be eradicated from my life,
that I may open myself to others and become a
channel of your gracious and everlasting love
to them.
I can't do this through my feeble efforts;
only you can accomplish such a change in my life.
Do it, Lord, whatever the cost or consequence;
for I truly want to be your disciple and servant
as long as I am permitted to live in this world.

5 ———————————There
R Is Always Hope

omans 15:4-13 "Everything that was written in the past was written to teach [you], so that through endurance and the encouragement of the Scriptures [you] might have hope" (v. 4).

Christians would probably like to begin the day with a smattering of ecstasy and rise to their feet with happiness in their hearts and hallelujahs on their lips. There are those days, however, when they have to settle for hope. Spiritual ecstasies are, for most people, few and far between; but hope abounds forever. Even those dark days along the journey of faith are pregnant with hope. Behind the heavy clouds that threaten is the sun that will eventually burn them away to flood dull lives with light and joy. Thus there is hope; always there is hope.

The Scriptures encourage and give hope—as do the lives of countless saints throughout history and many of those who walk the same journey with you today. God loves you; Christ has come to declare and demonstrate that love. You may not always feel this to be true; it is true nonetheless. This is the source of that everlasting joy that overcomes your struggles with depression and undergirds your life with a peace that is not swept away by the tempests of this daily existence.

Christians are able to begin each day with praises on their lips—no matter how heavy their hearts. Because you are a fallible human being in a disjointed world, this may not always be possible. Nevertheless, even if you cannot break into ecstasy , you can have hope; and there are those days when hope is enough.

Prayer for the Day

Thank you for keeping me through the night, O
God.
You have forgiven me the sins and errors of yesterday.
Now I am privileged to begin a new day,
   to start over again,
   to step out into this world as your child and
   servant assigned to serve in your purposes.
I praise you for the assurance that,
   as you watch over your own through the night,
   you will walk with me through each day.
I dedicate this day to you, O Lord,
   that I may travel in that course you set before me.
Help me to be faithful and obedient to your hope
   before me and to the voice of your Spirit
   within me,
   and allow my morning praises to continue
   throughout this day,
   reflecting your love and glory
   in all my relationships and activities.

6 ——————The Time Is Short

1 Corinthians 7:29-31   "What I mean, brothers, is that the time is short" (v. 29).

No one knows the year or the day, but you are nearer to the end of this dispensation and the time of Christ's return than you have ever been. You need to consider your priorities, and to be aware that earthly relationships and matters are not to have priority over the matters of the Spirit, those kingdom matters for which God has made each of his children responsible.

Your relationship to God has first priority. Proceeding from this, your relationship to your fellow beings is of vital importance. Whether God's children are happy or sad, rich or poor, famous or unknown in respect to this world will not matter in the end. Their primary concern must be their relationship to God, to "seek first his kingdom and his righteousness." This means that you seek to be what Jesus—and Paul—exhort you to be. They call you to be a light in this dark world (Matthew 5:14, Ephesians 5:8), and to love God and also love your neighbors as yourself (Matthew 22:37-39). Rely on God to work through you in showing love and being a light.

Seeking God's kingdom first is not always rational or reasonable in your kind of society and culture. God's gift of eternal life and your inclusion in his eternal kingdom are not comprehensible to earth-bound minds. Nevertheless, you can keep reaching toward that glorious freedom that enables you to soar over and above the entanglements that hold you so close to this planet. You have been created for far better things.

Prayer for the Day

This is your day, O Lord.
You made it; it belongs to you.
And yet you share it with me,
    with all of its opportunities and challenges,
    its problems and risks.
I thank you for your day, O Lord,
    and for whatever it may bring my way.
Keep me from becoming entrapped in its snares,
    its corruptions and pitfalls.
It is the first day of the rest of my life;
    it could also be the last day of my
    life on this earth.
Enable me to be faithful to you on this day
    in order that I may reign with you for eternity.
Even while I labor in the valley,
    may I lift my eyes to the cloud-shrouded,
    snow-capped peaks that hover over its edges,
    and be reminded that I am your child
    and your servant forever.
This is your day, O Lord.
Help me to live it in accordance
    with your plan and will for my life.

7———You Have Been Blessed

phesians 1:3-14 "Praise be to the God and Father of our Lord Jesus Christ, who has blessed [you] in the heavenly realms with every spiritual blessing in Christ" (v. 3).

You have much to celebrate as a child of God. You have through Jesus Christ become the recipient of God's whole treasure-house of spiritual gifts. Before the world itself was created, you were destined to be a child of God.

Christ's death on the cross set you free from the law's demands. All charges against you were blotted out. Your sins were forgiven. Reconciled to the divine family, you are now an integral part of God's plan to reconcile the whole world to himself. It is not something you can fully understand, but God created you to be his child and this was God's purpose and plan from the very beginning. This is made known to you and made possible for you through Jesus Christ. Through this Christ and his indwelling Spirit, the brand of God's ownership was burned indelibly into your heart. The gift of the Spirit is the guarantee that all of these gifts, even those presently unseen and little understood, are already yours and will be revealed in God's own time.

May the Spirit of God break through the dimness of your perception and reveal to you something of who you are and what you have become through Christ. He is Lord over all, and you are a member of his church—his body, the extension of his kingdom in the world to which you are assigned. How immeasurably and infinitely blessed you are!

Prayer for the Day

*Y*ou have granted me another day, O Lord.
Yesterday, with its wasted opportunities and
selfish enterprises, is gone forever.
It may be that today won't be much different, Lord.
But it could be, if I stay within your orbit
    for my life and run your errands even as I
    recognize my appointment and commitment
    as your servant in your world.
So be it, Lord; this is truly what I want.
Because of me, or in spite of me,
    may your love touch some lonely, needy person
    today.
I no longer want to build empires,
    to ascend thrones,
    or to be number one in my little kingdom.
I want to love you
    and respond to your love for me
    by communicating such love to others.
I want to use the precious gifts of life,
    freedom, and spiritual power
    as I relate to people
    by your grace to draw them into your
    kingdom of light and love.
This is what I want, O Lord.
May the victory today be yours.

8————Love and Compassion

*C*olossians 3:12-17 "Therefore, as [one of] God's chosen people, holy and dearly loved, clothe your[self] with compassion, kindness, humility, gentleness and patience" (v. 12).

The apostle Paul challenges God's children with a large order, one that is impossible to fill save by the grace of a loving God. Nevertheless, you *are* God's child. In response to God's redeeming act on your behalf and the gift of the Spirit, you are empowered and expected to reflect the qualities and attributes of the family of God.

It doesn't come naturally, these qualities revealed by Jesus Christ. Your body and mind are still earthbound and constantly subject to temptations that afflict you and are difficult to resist. A total dedication to God and his purposes, with a determination to live as the Lord would have you live, is essential in the daily struggle of allowing the Spirit to work in you.

Above all is the high challenge of loving. It is by means of God's love through you that others in your path may be introduced to God's saving grace. You may think that the call to love others means sending large amounts of money to groups that help people. It can include that, but love needs to take on a minute-by-minute flavor. This can involve being friendly with a check-out clerk, forgiving your children, smiling at a neighbor, and being kind to those around you. Love is a way of being that God calls you to exemplify.

God provides the grace and the enablement to do this. You must provide the fertile soil in which God's sown seeds may bring forth fruit.

Prayer for the Day

I am grateful, my loving God,
    for my arena of service,
    for a place to put my feet,
    for burdens to carry and lives to touch
    in the course of my daily labors.
May I be sensitive to your leading and to
    the hurts and needs of people around me.
I step into this day as your messenger and servant.
Help me to be bold, yet full of understanding,
    steeped in conviction, yet humble and tolerant
    of the convictions of others,
    willing to proclaim, yet just as willing to listen,
    and ready always to reach out
    to someone who is lost and lonely.
Grant to me, O God, the grace to be compassionate
    in my relationship to
    my brothers and sisters about me, to show
    kindness and love to everyone in my path.
And while I am your servant,
    may I be a student as well,
    willing to learn and to grow
    in my understanding of life
    and your purposes in the world about me.

9 ———— From Griping to Gratitude

1 Thessalonians 5:16-24 "Be joyful always; pray continually; give thanks in all circumstances . . ." (vv. 16-18).

Perhaps Paul does sound a bit fanatical. In view of the pain and misery that circumvents this world, how can one rejoice? In the midst of the fast-paced and fast-lane living, and the innumerable, unreasonable demands that plague people today, how is it possible to be continuously engaged in prayer? And to "give thanks in all circumstances"? It seems utterly unrealistic. Yet Paul says "this is God's will for you in Christ Jesus."

Paul did not have rocks in his head; he had Christ in his heart. He discovered amidst the many hard-knock experiences of this life that it was possible to be joyful and thankful even in the face of the dire circumstances.

Viktor Frankl in his book, *Man's Search for Meaning*, describes the conditions in a concentration camp during World War II. One freedom after another was denied, but Frankl noted the one that could not be taken away was their freedom to choose how to see things. He and others chose to see good in spite of the evil all around them, to see God at work in the midst of suffering.

"God's will" for you is not the ugly circumstances you confront; it is the kind of abiding in Christ and relationship of love and trust in him that is demonstrated in rejoicing, prayer, and thanksgiving, despite the conditions of this world. The amazing consequence of such trust—and this is beyond human comprehension—is the way God turns many of these difficult circumstances into a means of accomplishing his divine purposes in and through his beloved children and servants.

Prayer for the Day

My loving God,
you have turned my griping into gratitude,
my groans of despair into proclamations of joy.
How can I help but explode with praises and
vow to spend eternity in giving thanks to you?
You are my hope and salvation,
my morning sun and evening star,
my shade in the desert heat,
my warmth in the cold of the night.
You are the Bread of Life when I am hungry,
and a life-giving spring
when my soul is parched and dry.
You are the answer to my agonizing questions,
the fulfillment of my deepest longings.
I am yours, O God, yours forever.
Make my life a perpetual offering of praise.

10—The Coming Dawn

*R*omans 13:11-14   "The hour has come for you to wake up from your slumber, because [your] salvation is nearer now than when [you] first believed" (v. 11).

Now is the time to get up and "clothe your[self] with the Lord Jesus Christ. . . . the night is nearly over; the day is almost here," wrote Paul, and that is about as close as he comes to making any predictions in respect to Christ's coming and the final ingathering of God's children into his eternal kingdom.

While Paul warned against date setting, and even reprimanded some of his readers for giving up their jobs and normal responsibilities to thumb-twiddle on some holy hill awaiting Christ's promised return, he was filled with anticipation concerning that great and ultimate event.

In the meantime, God's children are to live and act as if his kingdom has already been revealed, the sun already risen, for even while there is darkness and devastation about you, Christ *has* come, the kingdom of God *is* here. You are to "put aside the deeds of darkness" and live and love, minister and serve, as God's sons and daughters are destined to do. This news of the coming dawn ought to help you dispel your fears and fill your being with joy as you continue on the journey of faith.

Prayer for the Day

Thank you, my loving God, for another day.
I don't know what adventures it holds for me.
I may be surprised by joy,
   or wounded by pain or sorrow.
Help me to be thankful in all circumstances,
   to believe that no matter what comes my way,
   you are with me,
   my refuge and strength.
Grant, O God, that I approach this day
   as your child—without doubt or fear,
   knowing that whatever happens,
   my relationship to you is never in jeopardy.
And grant that I may be able
   to bring your love and joy
   into any difficult circumstances
   that confront me.

11————————The Risk
of Loving

L̶uke 20:9-18 "I will send my son, whom I love; perhaps they will respect him" (v. 13).

The parable Jesus related reveals something of the risk of loving. The owner of the vineyard sent a servant, a second, then a third servant to the tenants of his vineyard to bring back some of its fruits. The servants were beaten and thrown out. Then the owner sent his son— but the tenants killed him. Most of God's human creatures have thus responded to God's love from that time to this by rejecting his Son, Jesus Christ. Yet the God of love refuses to let go or give up; he continues the risk of loving. He keeps on loving even those who reject his overtures—even until they break and possibly destroy themselves by their own resistance. "While we were still sinners, Christ died for us" (Rom. 5:8b).

The God who took such a risk on your behalf expects that you begin to take some risks on behalf of your fellow beings. You have a position of trust and responsibility in the vineyard of the Master; it is to love your brothers and sisters in the human family. This is meant to be your primary vocation in life. There is, indeed, a risk in this kind of loving. And there are those whom you love who are incapable of understanding, accepting, or returning such love.

Loving others can involve a measure of pain and suffering, certainly some discomfort and inconvenience. At the same time, even if there is no response to your love, the very effort to love stretches your soul and enlarges your capacity for enrichment. "Anyone who does not love remains in death," wrote John. At least you are truly alive when you reach out to love.

Prayer for the Day

Gracious heavenly Father,
you have sent your Son to reveal your love
for your creatures upon this world,
and you have thereby delivered me from sin's
deathly grasp and reconciled me to your kingdom.
May that love impel me to risk loving and thereby
relate the knowledge and experience of
your love to others about me.
I pray that you may somehow reach those
I couldn't love or make to feel my love.
Grant that I may truly learn how to love
others as you love me
and thereby communicate your love to lonely,
despairing people in my path.
Heal the wounds of anyone I may have hurt today
and enrich the lives of those I may have helped.
Enable me to love freely and deeply even if there
appears to be no response to my love.
Thank you for your eternal love, O Lord.
Now grant me the courage, the wisdom,
and the willingness to risk loving others
with whom I come in contact—
and to do so regardless of the consequences
to my life.

12 ———— From Futility to Fulfillment

ohn 4:5-26 "Whoever drinks the water I give him will never thirst" (v. 14).

Back of the glitter and painted scenery out front of most people's lives, there is naked reality—often disorder, confusion, and excruciating futility. Many feel a bit like Cosette in Victor Hugo's *Les Miserables*, tugging away at her heavy bucket, wishing deeply that she could "fly, to fly with all her might, across woods, across fields, to houses, to windows, to lighted candles." The message of John's gospel is that futility can give way to fulfillment, that God has taken upon himself the heavy load with which people are so frantically struggling, that there can be meaning and value, point and purpose in their daily conflicts.

Jesus began his ministry to the Samaritan woman by making her conscious of the futility in her heart and life. He then reached out to offer her fulfillment. She had come to the well for the purpose of drawing water. What she found at the well was water of a different sort—a new heart, a new life. She met Jesus, and she became a new creature.

"My soul thirsts for the living God," said David. It was true with David; so it is with you. The basis for most futility is the thirst in people's lives for the living water which Christ offers so freely. You need only to cease culling your comfort and consolation from some abstract, unknown God, and consecrate yourself to God revealed in Jesus Christ, and to receive from him, delight in him, love and serve him. Then your futility will give way to fulfillment.

Prayer for the Day

My soul finds rest in God alone . . .
 he alone is my rock and my salvation,"
 exclaimed the psalmist.
"My soul thirsts for you where there is no water."
This is also my cry and my prayer, dear Lord.
This life, this journey apart from you is
 indeed utter futility.
Whether it be an Olympic medal, a published book,
 an educational degree, a lottery win,
 a high position—whatever,
 by itself, none of these things can bring
 long-lived or eternal fulfillment.
They cannot stand the test of time.
They bring little comfort or security when the
 journey becomes dark and lonely,
 and the future is without hope.
You are my Shepherd, O Lord,
 and I shall not want
 even if it appears at times that you are absent
 from the fold or the world you have created.
It is from you that I draw the juice of life.
It is in you that the deepest longings of my heart
 are met and my fulfillment is complete.

13————So You Feel Guilty

1 *John 1:5-10* "If we confess our sins, he is faithful and just and will forgive us our sins and purify us from all unrighteousness" (v. 9).

Guilt feelings rob people of pleasant memories of the past. They take the joy out of the present. They dim and obscure the future. They act like thorns in the flesh that scratch and prick people in the rose garden of happiness. They are like clouds that keep blotting out the sun—or like nagging demons that keep their victims feeling inferior and inadequate.

Guilt feelings are sometimes necessary and may move people to constructive action. For instance, having a little guilt about wastefulness might motivate some to recycle materials like newspapers and aluminum.

Some guilt feelings are imaginary, repressed, or even unrecognized, with no actual basis or benefit. Whatever the source or the purpose, they must be dealt with lest they stifle your effectiveness or sap your strength or cheat you out of the joy that enriches your life and relationships along the journey of faith.

"Therefore, there is now no condemnation for those who are in Christ Jesus," wrote Paul (Rom. 8:1). Here lies the cure for guilt. The conflicts that arise out of guilt may well serve to keep you open to the grace of God—and point to matters that need to be rectified. When you realize the significance of God's forgiveness and acceptance, you then can return to loving and accepting your family members and friends, and you can also discover meaning and purpose in your daily ambitions as well as your conflicts.

Prayer for the Day

I know, dear Lord, how foolish it is to allow my
memories of stupid and selfish things done in
the past to threaten my relationship to you and
deprive me of the joy I should experience
as I follow you.

I have confessed my sins and they are forgiven and
forgotten, according to your Word and promises.

Yet I think often about those people I may have
hindered in their relationship to you because of
something I did or neglected to do.

There are times when I have been self-centered and
lacked compassion for my family, friends, and fel-
low-workers.

I do try to serve you by being a servant to those
in need around me;
I feel so often that I fail.

Deliver me, O God, from those feelings that are
often the cause of failure in my
interpersonal relationships.

I claim anew your forgiveness, O God, knowing that
the joy and peace of a relationship with you
will replace my guilt feelings
and enable me to reflect joy in the
circumstances about me.

14————Love, Honor, and Forgive

Matthew 6:9-15 "If you do not forgive men their sins, your Father will not forgive your sins" (v. 15).

The old marriage vows used to read: "Love, honor, and obey." Perhaps they ought to read: "Love, honor, and forgive." A forgiving spirit begins with your acceptance of God's love and forgiveness. It must be followed—and this is implied in such acceptance—by your ability to forgive yourself. It is remarkable how often one's unforgiving attitudes toward others is in reality a reflection or a projection of disgust toward one's self. A humble and honest appraisal of yourself should certainly make you tender, accepting, understanding, and forgiving of your fellow human beings.

You are not expected to condone the wrongdoings of others any more than you are expected to condone your own. Yet you may have to learn how to tolerate the weaknesses of others until those weaknesses are transformed into strength and their liabilities are turned into assets.

Can you forgive others: a child who shuns the moral and spiritual values in which he or she has been reared? A spouse who can't respond to some of your childish needs? A friend who cons you out of your savings account? A drunk-driver who runs down a child? You are called to forgive, and you can—by God's enabling grace. "Forgive as the Lord forgave you," said Paul (Col. 3:13). While life goes on for the victim of your unforgiveness, a close relationship to your loving and forgiving heavenly Father is in jeopardy when you refuse to love and forgive.

Prayer for the Day

O Lord, you have forgiven me of so much,
   yet I am often incapable of truly forgiving others
   of some belligerent act or negative attitude
   toward me.
I say that I forgive others,
   yet my love for them is all but extinguished
   when something is said or done that threatens
   my feelings of self-concern or importance.
I can survive being snubbed or humbled by
   other people if I truly understand and accept
   your love and compassion for me.
Enable me to accept myself as you accept me—
   and then help me to risk being open and
   genuinely loving toward others despite
   what they may think about me.
Where there is hatred,
   help me to sow the seeds of love.
Where there are wounds,
   may I touch others with healing.
Where there is despair, help me to proclaim hope.
Where there is darkness, enable me to bring light.
Your grace, O God, has set me free from the need
   to make myself great and has helped me love others
   despite their inability to love me back.
Help me to love, honor, and forgive.

15 — Walking in the Light

Ephesians 5:8-14 "Live as children of light . . . and find out what pleases the Lord" (vv. 8-10).

Your immediate goal in respect to the day before you is not to please people; it is to please God. There is no guarantee that goal will please people about you, but it is the only way you can truly serve God and effectively communicate to the human family the grace and power of the living God. The way in which the divine and eternal light of God can be channeled into and focused upon the darkness that confounds and threatens the inhabitants of this planet is by way of God's children who "live as children of light."

The light that broke into the darkness of this world through Jesus Christ is now to be transmitted through God's redeemed children. This necessitates that they walk in the light, living as Jesus did, in honesty and openness, and in loving, self-denying concern for others.

This will not always be the popular thing to do. It means that you cannot participate in some of the everybody-does-it, shady, shadowy activities that others consider natural and necessary in their day-by-day existence. It may mean that you will have to make some controversial decisions and support some unpopular causes. It may, on the other hand, compel or encourage others around you to leave the dark paths of fruitless striving to discover Jesus as the Light of the World.

Prayer for the Day

Even if the sun never breaks through
the cloud cover,
and the path ahead appears to be dark
and foreboding,
it is my privilege and responsibility to walk
in the light of your righteousness, my Lord,
and to know that I will never go astray
as long as I abide in you, the Light of the World.
Thus I never need to be afraid,
nor do I ever have to be anxiety-ridden
or guilt-stricken, or desperately lonely,
or impeded by low worth or lack of self-esteem.
Thank you, dear God, for the Light that warms
and comforts and guides me along
the journey of faith.
Thank you for breaking through the distortions
and darkness of sin to prepare a way of salvation
for me and every human creature.
I commit myself to walking in your Light
this day, O Lord.
May I reflect that Light to others along the way
that their darkness may be dispelled
by your love and saving grace.

16———When Life Has Meaning

John 15:9-17 "You did not choose me, but I chose you to go and bear fruit—fruit that will last" (v. 16).

"He who has a *why* to live can bear almost any *how*," said an old philosopher. "Do not work for food that spoils, but for food that endures to eternal life," said Jesus. It is in the love and grace of God that empty souls find filling, guilty hearts find forgiveness, purposeless lives find a goal and design.

You need to acknowledge that you are a person of worth. Such significance is not due to something acquired or merited through personal effort. "I chose you and appointed you," said Jesus. It began with creation when the human being was made in the spiritual image of God. That image was abused and distorted by sin and self-centeredness. The Christian is restored to God and his purposes by means of the cross and the resurrection of Jesus Christ. You have been set free from sin's guilt and are now the recipient of God's saving grace. Thus you can no longer live for yourself; it would only lead you up blind alleys or down dead-end streets. "You are not your own; you were bought at a price," wrote Paul (1 Cor. 6:19b-20a).

Whether your work week is utilized in typing letters, collecting garbage, presiding over some corporation, or caring for children, genuine meaning for life is realized when you are dedicated to following Christ. You can carry out his purposes no matter what the arena is in which he leads you.

Prayer
for the Day

Dear Lord, it is difficult to believe that you chose
me to be your child and servant on this world
in which I have been born.
I do not have within me everything it takes
to meet the challenges of life about me,
or to make any worthwhile contributions
to my world or any of its inhabitants.
While some of my youthful aspirations were
generous and grandiose,
they were often fanciful and unrealistic as well.
They nevertheless did focus on one thing or another
and you graciously nurtured and shaped them
into less selfish objectives.
Eternal God, I need again and again to be
returned to your will for my life.
Forgive me for cluttering it up with
self-centered ambitions.
Restore me to your orbit and design for me.
May the sense of divine purpose and goal keep me
steady within and motivate me despite the
confusions and consternations I meet along
the journey of faith.

17——On a Doubt-filled Day

John 20:26-29 "Blessed are those who have not seen and yet have believed" (v. 29).

The resurrection of Jesus did not eliminate all the doubts of those who followed him. Even while Christians today seek to walk in trust and obedience, times of doubt occasionally plague those who are sincere truth-seekers along the journey of faith. Doubting Thomas was by no means a pathetically weak figure in those exciting days following the resurrection event. After all, he did not actually witness the resurrection of his Lord and Master, and unlike his comrades, he had not as yet seen the risen Christ; neither have the multitudes of followers and faith-journey travelers since that time. Yet they were privileged to look over the shoulders of those early Christians and discover that the "Doubting Thomas" incident is meaningful for them.

There appears to be a special blessing for "those who have not seen and yet have believed." You can have a faith that makes you willing to risk asking piercing questions and lay yourself on the line every day whether God seems near or far away. The doubts that assail you today may well lead you tomorrow to a faith that is bolder and stronger than you ever dreamed possible. "Doubting Thomas" becomes a believing Thomas with the declaration: "My Lord and my God!" The words of Jesus are graciously addressed to you and to all who press on through life's storms and uncertainties: "Blessed are those who have not seen and yet have believed"—and who willingly lay themselves on the line every day whether God seems near or far away.

Prayer for the Day

Father in heaven, all-loving and ever-merciful,
there are those days when I wonder
what life is all about,
and there are those times when you seem to be
absent from the world you created and
the creatures you love.
My faith in you,
your great acts and wonderful promises,
sometimes gives way to frustrating questions
about the Holocaust, the oppressed populations of
various nations, the poor, the enslaved, the
tortured, the diseased, even the dying children
who are crying out your name.
I know that most ugly atrocities that destroy
vast numbers of your children are caused by
ignorant and hate-filled people,
yet so many suffer and die amidst calamities
and disasters that are not caused by human beings.
I know there are uncountable times throughout
history when you intervened on behalf of your
creatures to preserve them and to continue
carrying out your purposes on this planet.
Grant to me, O God, the faith that will continue
to serve you
whether you seem near or far away,
and grant the faith that will embrace you despite
unanswered questions that sometimes haunt me.

18————————The Call
of Christ

Matthew 9:9-13 "[Jesus] saw a man named Matthew sitting at the tax collector's booth. 'Follow me,' he told him, and Matthew got up and followed him" (v. 9).

The most astounding, incredible fact of all history is the call of Christ to sinful men and women, the invitation to follow him. It is extended to all, including the most unpromising creatures on the face of the earth. No matter how failure-fraught or inadequate you think you are, you are invited to follow Jesus Christ, to become a son or daughter of God, a servant and disciple of your Savior and Lord.

This is not an invitation to casual acquaintance or weekly worship. It is not an offer of outside help when you are on the hot-seat. It is the call to follow him, to love him, serve him, and crown him Lord of every phase and facet, attitude and aspect of your life. This means a dedication to the purposes as well as to the Person of Christ, to loving, serving, and giving yourself for the humanity that he came to save and to serve.

Of course you *accept* Jesus Christ. This ought to flood your life with the joy of sin forgiven and the assurance of life eternal. If you, however, are to be effective as a Christian and obedient as a son or daughter of God, you must *follow* Jesus Christ. You may not know where he will lead you. You can be assured that such a course will compel and enable you to reach out in love toward your fellow creatures about you.

It is a joyful and fulfilling life.

Prayer for the Day

I know, Lord, that I have always belonged to you.
I know, as well, that I have sometimes acted as if
 I didn't, and have, instead, sauntered off
 thinking that happiness and adventure were
 somewhere out there among the bright lights
 and rollicking crowds.
I am lonely, Lord, because some of my
 friends are not with me in the faith;
 and I feel alien to this world and all it
 appears to offer.
Yet I am grateful for your invitation to follow you,
 and for leading me to the decision and
 determination to surrender my life to you
 and your purposes.
My heart is filled with joy—
 the kind that bright lights and rollicking
 crowds can never offer.
This joy is ample reward for responding
 to your call to service.
I pray, O God, that you will never give up on me,
 that I will continue to hear clearly and respond
 gratefully to your call to loving obedience.
Grant, my Savior and Master,
 that I be faithful to you.
I want to be your child and servant wherever
 you may lead me regardless of the trials
 and tribulations that come my way.

19———Some People You Can't Love

Luke 7:36-48 "He who has been forgiven little loves little" (v. 47).

You find it difficult to love certain people. While it is usually easy to respond to those who love you—and are even eager to return affection and adoration to those who meet your needs, it is not as easy for you to love those who do not gratefully receive your love or do not love in return.

"Anyone who does not love remains in death," wrote John (1 John 3:14b). He is saying in effect: love—and possibly get hurt; cease loving—and cease living. "This is how we know what love is: Jesus Christ laid down his life for us. And we ought to lay down our lives for our brothers," said John (1 John 3:16). This kind of love has its origin in God alone. You can portray it or witness to it only as far as you receive and abide in God's love.

Great is that love that is capable of accepting you despite your sins, that love of your God who takes upon himself the consequences of your wrongdoings and reconciles you and reinstates you in his love and purposes! It is only in the measure that you accept God's eternal love that you are enabled to truly love others.

Prayer for the Day

I have discovered, O Lord,
   that despite my enthusiastic affirmations and
   proclamations of your love for humankind,
   there are some people I do not like very much.
I have no problem with those who affirm
   and support me.
When it comes to people who attempt to use me,
   or have no use for me,
   or even have the audacity to question
   or criticize my actions,
   I feel very little love or concern for them.
While you love and accept me as I am,
   even when I fail you or cease to serve you,
   I am not capable of loving and accepting
   those who do not in some measure serve me.
As far as I fail to love, I fail to serve you.
I am often selfish and self-centered,
   concerned primarily about my own
   station and status in life.
I have often been using you, my loving God,
   to fulfill my aspirations rather than to
   discover wholeness and fulfillment
   in submitting myself to your loving control.
Forgive me, O God, and teach me anew
   the meaning of your great love.
Teach me how to love and accept others
   as you love and accept me.

20———————Courage
to Live

John 14:1-6 "Do not let your hearts be troubled. Trust in God; trust also in me" (v. 1).

Someone said that "anxiety is the result of not knowing who we are and to whom we belong." But you know who you are and to whom you belong. You even know your eternal goal. Yet you are anxious about many things. Maybe you are looking at the wind rather than the Lord of the wind, or fear the waves that threaten to overwhelm you rather than confidently relying upon the Creator of those rushing waters. You are tossed around by the tumult about you and torn by the contradictions within you.

You may not be able to ignore the storm that rages or escape the conflicts that beset you or turn away from the heavy burdens that tax your strength. You can, however, focus anew on that One who is in the midst of the storm, who will stand with you through the conflict and who will not bend under the weight of heavy burdens.

Recognize anew your identity: "We are the children of God," declared John. Reestablish your confidence in God's continual presence: "Even though I walk through the valley of the shadow of death, I will fear no evil, for you are with me," proclaimed the psalmist. Affirm God's promises: "You will grieve, but your grief will turn to joy," said Jesus.

St. Teresa of Avila once said: "The further I journey in life—God help me—the less comfort I find." Nor will you find a great deal of "comfort" in a traditional sense on the journey of faith, but you will always have the grace of God to support and sustain you, and give you peace.

Prayer for the Day

I live, O God, in a churning, conflict-ridden,
revolutionary world.
This is frightening at times, and my reaction
is a retreat to the sanctuary of the past
where I assume I can be free from
the everyday tensions of this life.
I look to the church where I hear
those great words about my security and safety
in you.
Yet you forbid, Lord,
that I run away from this crisis.
You came to "set fire to the earth,"
and revolution is, in part,
a consequence of your Word to us.
You have placed me in the midst of crises, O God.
They are all about me.
Help me, undergirded by your grace,
filled with your Spirit,
to find my place in a revolutionary world,
to put my reputation, job, income, even my life,
on the line to confront violence with courage
and hatred with love,
to be your faithful child and servant
in the midst of crises.
Grant to me the courage to stand firm and
to be confident whatever the conflicts
and contradictions I face in this world.

21——The Graciousness
of Uncertainty

John 3:1-3 "What we will be has not yet been made known" (v. 2).

Before one can recognize the "graciousness of uncertainty," according to Oswald Chambers, he or she must first know the One Great Certainty. Thomas the doubting disciple expresses uncertainty: "How can we know the way?" Jesus presents himself as Certainty: "I am the way and the truth and the life." Most people look upon uncertainty as a bad thing. They assume they have to reach a certain goal or accomplish a particular objective. The Christian increasingly discovers that following Christ is not always a matter of common sense, and the risks that he or she is invited to take will often appear to be downright foolish.

Uncertainties may plague you on all sides. If your eyes are focused upon the things or values of this world, there will be tremor and trepidation. The uncertainties of life on this planet will continue to haunt you and this often leads to depression and sometimes to despair.

"What we will be has not yet been made known," wrote John, but he quickly and emphatically declares: "*Now* we are children of God. . . . How great is the love the Father has lavished on us, that we should be called children of God."

There is that One whom sin has not touched and the uncertainties of this world have not overcome. He, Jesus Christ, remains the One Great Certainty. A total commitment to him removes the fear and frustration of this life's uncertainties and makes the journey of faith one of joy and excitement despite the "unknowns" and the many perplexities and difficulties along the way.

Prayer for the Day

Dear Lord, I know all the words designed to comfort and assure.
I am aware of your promise to stay close beside me
whatever the crisis that confronts me.
And yet there are innumerable uncertainties that plague
me and leave me disturbed and anxious,
and sometimes I find the joy
of my commitment to you
losing its glow and affecting my witness
to my family and friends.
Forgive me, O Lord, when my faith is small and my
doubts are large, and when I allow my heart to be
taken up with uncertainties about me.
Help me instead to focus upon you,
the One Great Certainty.
You have promised sufficient grace for special trials.
I lay claim to that grace.
Enable me to sense your loving presence undergirding
and overseeing my life over and above these
uncertainties in my mind and heart.

22———From One Beggar to Another

Matthew 20:20-28 "Whoever wants to become great among you must be your servant" (v. 26).

Teach us to walk on water, Lord;
They'll applaud us, far and wide.
Such miracles won't help the world,
But they would increase our pride.

Don't send us out to feed the flock;
The kids step on our toes;
The bread gets dry; the fish might smell;
And the baskets snag our clothes.

This little piece of poetry speaks more emphatically and directly than do many sermons from many pulpits. Daniel Niles defined evangelism as "One beggar telling another beggar where to find bread." When all who follow Jesus Christ as their Savior and Lord become his disciples, they also become evangelists. Wisdom, influence, nobility are not the basic ingredients for successful evangelism. You come to the mercy seat of God as a beggar to receive from him the Bread of Life. While so many newborn children of God are seeking special miracles or gifts which seldom do little more than exalt themselves, God is choosing beggars and is using them to carry out his purposes in this world.

Even while you are a royal son or daughter of God, you are yet a beggar who is perpetually sustained by the Bread of God's infinite grace. You are also royally commissioned to the splendid task of leading other beggars to that grand Source of life and joy.

Prayer for the Day

I thank you, my loving God, that I am eligible for
your life-redeeming grace,
that you love spiritual beggars such as I,
and can grant them your righteousness and
equip them for service in your kingdom.
This is the only reason I dare to come to you,
so that I can discover meaning and purpose for
my life in my relationship to you.
You have accepted me as a beggar and turned me
into a child of your eternal kingdom.
You have granted me "every spiritual blessing in Christ."
You indwell my life through your Holy Spirit and
entrust me with the blessed task of telling
other beggars where they can find the Bread of Life
and how they may become
your royal sons and daughters
and of even leading them to the foot of the cross,
the empty tomb, and the grand experience
of everlasting life.
To you, O Father, who are able to do immeasurably more
[even for us beggars] than all we even dare ask, be
the glory forever and ever.

23——The Importance of Being Imperfect

2 Corinthians 12:1-10 "My grace is sufficient for you, for my power is made perfect in weakness" (v. 9).

Before you can accept the imperfections of others, you must learn how to accept your own. This does not mean that you cherish or condone them, but that you recognize them and are always aware of them. The failure to do that gives these distortions the power to cripple you and render you ineffective in the matter of serving your fellow beings.

Your imperfections do not subtract from or diminish your value and significance as a person. They do not have to be your undoing. They can even be useful in directing you toward proper self-acceptance and enable you to more lovingly relate to others around you. This will happen only if you have the courage to face up to your imperfections, accept them as a part of your sin-permeated human nature, and deal with them with your endowed intelligence and the grace made available to you in Jesus Christ.

"By one sacrifice he has made perfect forever those who are being made holy," wrote the author of the Letter to the Hebrews. The perfection God requires can never be a matter of personal achievement. This is a gift—and must be received as such. It is received, not by personal effort or endeavor, but by receiving Jesus Christ.

Actually, it's your imperfections that make you eligible for God's loving grace and forgiveness as communicated to you through the Word and the Sacraments. It is God's perfection that is shared with you as you respond in faith to Jesus Christ.

Prayer for the Day

O God, I am often belabored and weighed down
by my weaknesses and imperfections.
Sometimes I don't feel I have the abilities or talents
to do what I am expected to do.
Yet you have not only redeemed and restored me to
your family as your child,
but I am to be your servant and I am to serve
you by loving my brothers and
sisters about me.
I thank you, my God, because there is no question
as to my eligibility for your grace and
forgiveness.
I am a fallible human being,
yet I am the object of your love and concern
and the recipient of your grace and power
to carry out your purposes along
the journey of faith.
I thank you, O God, because despite my imperfections,
you have granted me value and significance
as your beloved child and servant.
Help me to give to others the right to be imperfect
and to offer to them the kind of love and
acceptance you have granted me.

24 ———————God Loves Failures

*R*omans 11:32-36 "God has bound all men over to disobedience so that he may have mercy on them all" (v. 32).

The psalmist knew the meaning of failure: "He lifted me out of the slimy pit, out of the mud and mire; he set my feet on a rock" (Ps. 40:2). Failure must have been a part of Paul's experience: "What a wretched man I am!" he wrote, "Who will rescue me from this body of death?" (Rom. 8:24). He knew the answer: "Thanks be to God— through Jesus Christ our Lord!" "I am unclean," was the admission of the leper to Christ. It was one of the prerequisites for being made clean. "I am unworthy," confessed the centurion. It was the beginning of a great miracle in his life. "I said, 'I will confess my transgressions to the Lord,' and you forgave the guilt of sin," cried David.

So you have failed. Failure can be the threshold to success. The fact of failure often slays self-sufficiency and prepares the way for faith. It is your faith in the grace and power of God through Christ that sets the stage for effectual and contributive living in your relationships to the people around you.

You are acceptable to God, for God loves failures. God can accomplish his purpose in your life despite your failures. It is God's miracle-working power that can turn your failures into successes.

Prayer for the Day

Lord, I've failed again.
   Despite my firm resolutions and determined efforts, I have flopped—fallen on my face.
Thus I am crawling back to you once more
   begging for forgiveness and reconciliation.
Sometimes I am a blundering idiot, O Lord.
I try to love—and I love unwisely.
I try to be selfless and generous—
   and I am suckered out of my savings.
I try to touch others with compassionate concern,
   and my knuckles get wrapped with scorn.
I try to communicate the message of your grace
   and judgment, and it is thrown right back
   into my teeth.
Thus I come in supplication back to you again.
Keep my failings from threatening or
   hurting others about me.
Forgive me, O God, and when I fail, help me
   remember that you accept me fully
   through your Son Jesus Christ. Guide me,
   empower me, and work through me to reach
   others with your promise of love and forgiveness.

25————Discipleship
and Involvement

John 20:19-23 "As the Father has sent me, I am sending you" (v. 21).

Jesus calls us to discipleship. Discipleship means involvement. Our Lord set the pace, and he expects his disciples to keep it. He identified himself with the agonies of humankind. He became involved in their crying needs. He even went so far as to bear the consequences of their sins. To be a disciple of Christ means that you who accept him as your Savior must also accept him as your Lord and Master. To follow him means that you continue in his course for your life. It's not enough to criticize the corruption of your society from the pews and pulpits of your churches; you are expected to become involved in the blood and tears, sorrows and sufferings of God's creatures in suburb and ghetto, mainstreet and marketplace, wherever they may be found.

Because you are involved in the sickness of this world, you must, as a disciple of Christ, become involved in its cure. Often this is not convenient or comfortable; it might even be dangerous. You may have to risk your health, wealth, reputation or status, even your very life in this involvement.

Discipleship means involvement. As your Lord gave himself on your behalf, you are expected to give yourself on behalf of others, even to lose your life in service to others. But that is when you find it anew in the incomparable joy of being a child and servant of the living and everlasting God.

Prayer for the Day

Loving Christ, you identified with me in my sins
   and sicknesses.
You adopted me as your child and commissioned me
   to be your servant.
I need your help to fulfill my servanthood by
   identifying with the needs of my brothers
   and sisters and in communicating your love and
   grace to them.
I understand that my response to your great love
   must be commitment.
Discipleship will not lead to softness and may lead
   to suffering.
I am learning, my Lord,
   that my service to you must be rendered
   to your human creatures about me.
I am to be, in some amazing manner,
   a visible member of your divine personhood.
O God, you have entrusted me with an
   awesome responsibility.
Enable me, by your grace, to be your
   faithful and effective servant.

26 —————————Sinners Need a Savior

Luke 5:17-32 "I have not come to call the righteous, but sinners to repentance" (v. 32).

If you are up against something that is too much for you; if there are problems, weaknesses, sins in your life that you cannot solve or overcome; if you are lost in the wilderness of your own failures and insufficiencies— then you are ready for outside help. Only when the prodigal son was at the end of his rope, backed up against the wall, did he come to his senses; he "got up and went to his father." It is "impossible for a man of himself to escape," said Seneca, "it must be that someone stretch forth a hand to draw him out."

The gospel of Jesus Christ proclaims that he is seeking "the one who is lost." Not until a person realizes that he or she is lost, that there is no escape, no way out, will that person cry out for deliverance. The very purpose of Christ's coming, the cross, the empty tomb, the churches that abound throughout the world, is to reach out to those who need help, who need deliverance from the road or the life that goes nowhere, who need to be rescued from the sin which blinds and the disease that destroys. Where there is no recognized sin, no unsolved problems, no moral or human weaknesses, people feel little need for a Savior.

The Great Physician stands near to heal and deliver and forgive and empower. He will grant you the courage and strength and wisdom you so much need to overcome those overwhelming problems along your journey—and the grace to discover God's direction and purpose for your life.

Prayer for the Day

Great God, I am made of such frail stuff.
I am often restless, unsatisfied;
>my every nerve reaches out for tangible thrill
>and sensual support.

At those times your promises of joy and strength seem
>vague,
>obscure,
>unreachable.

My sins accelerate; my faith shrivels.
I am simply not the stuff of which saints are made.
When I feel empty and inadequate,
>I cannot sense your power or presence.

Is it possible the saints of old felt
>the same way at times?

That they also were plagued with human
>weakness and frail flesh?

That they fell on their faces in foolish despair?
And yet their lives channeled your strength.
Their words communicated your Word.
Their deeds manifested your love.
I hear little about their defeats,
>but their victories are broadcast
>to every generation.

Grant, O God, that my frail stuff might become
>staunch material that can bless and benefit
>the lives of others about me today.

27————————Under New Orders

John 21:1-14 "Throw your net on the right side of the boat" (v. 6).

The excitement had subsided. The Christ who died on the cross had been raised from the dead. He had appeared to the disciples but was presently absent from them. "I am going fishing," said Peter. "We'll go with you," responded the other disciples. Off they went to the routine business of making a living.

That night, however, "they caught nothing." This summarizes the post-Easter experiences of so many people. They basked in the joy and beauty of Easter. Most of them believe with all their hearts that Jesus arose from the dead. On Monday they were back to their humdrum jobs. It was business as usual—with the same defeats, anxieties, and bondages, as the week before.

"Throw your net on the right side of the boat," called out a stranger on the beach. The disciples did what they were told and immediately caught a large quantity of fish. "It is the Lord!" cried John, and Peter leaped out of the boat to greet his Master.

Is it possible that this is the answer to your lackadaisical, impoverished, post-Easter activities? Do you need to rediscover Christianity in terms of a personal and vital relationship with the living Christ? If you do, you may still go back to your "fishing nets," but you go back under new orders. When you dedicate yourself to the principles and prerequisites of the living Christ and allow him to have his way in your life, the Christ of Easter will transform and empower you for post-Easter living.

Prayer for the Day

*E*ternal God,
   you who brought back Christ from the dead,
      resurrect through Christ this poor spirit of mine.
I do not seek to be delivered from the difficult
      circumstances I may face today,
         but I pray that the Spirit of the living Christ
         may be manifest in my everyday routine
         and activities.
Is it really true that the same power that raised
      Jesus Christ from the dead
         is the same power that you through your Spirit
         have given to me?
         That your indwelling is as real in me as it was
         in God-incarnate, Jesus Christ?
Is it true, Lord? You have said as much.
Help me to act as if it is true
      regardless of feelings or childish faith.
Grant to me, O God, the grace to respond
      to your love, your gifts, and your assignment
      as your servant,
         to live a valid Christian life as your child
         and servant in these days.

28————Mark of a True Disciple

John 13:34-35 "All men will know that you are my disciples if you love one another" (v. 35).

"As I have loved you, so you must love one another," said Jesus. Loving one's fellow human beings is the inevitable expression of true faith and, according to Jesus Christ, is the clearest evidence of an individual's Christianity. Your neighbor is God's representative in this sin-ridden world, and is selected by God to receive the love and service which you offer to God through your neighbor. The gifts granted to you are to be passed on to others. You are called to be Christ to your neighbor.

How, then, can you love your neighbor as Christ loves you? The springs of such love are in God, not in you. Even if your neighbor does not respond to God's love flowing through you, it will at least flow freely in your soul. It doesn't come naturally; it is something God empowers you to do. There are hazards and risks involved. It means that you become vulnerable. You may even break your own heart in the process.

There is, of course, an alternative. You may imprison yourself in the suffocating prison of your own selfishness—and never know the hurt of love rejected or the pain and price of sharing yourself with others. But never to know God's love or to express that love to others is the shortest and most certain road to hell—in this life as well as in the next.

Prayer for the Day

O Lord, in obedience to your Father's will
and in love for each of us as God's creatures,
you entered our wilderness and submitted
to the agony and misery of this earthly domain.
Such is the measure of your love for us.
When I look upon your cross,
    I discover in its terrible pain
    the peace of forgiven sin,
    and the freedom to live in loving relationships
    with my brothers and sisters about me.
I discover, as well, that I am also
    called to give myself for others,
    that there is a cross for me to bear
    in my journey through this life;
    that you who have set me free from sin's bondage
    have now returned to this wilderness
    to walk with me on my journey.
O Lord, I pray that you will turn these small or
    large sufferings that assail me into instruments of
    your redemption and channels of your love
    for those I touch on my pilgrimage
    through this world.

29——When One Thinks about Death

Psalm 23 "Even though I walk through the valley of the shadow of death, I will fear no evil, for you are with me" (v. 4).

A distinctly secular approach to the subject of death is well expressed in the words of Woody Allen: "I'm not afraid of death; I just don't want to be around when it happens." A writer more realistically and hopefully declares: "My life is a mystery, but death is a dark malady which faith cannot evade. Yet faith has a word; it speaks of process and purpose of which death is a part, and it speaks of something steady over all the wreckage." It is Jesus that, through proclamation and demonstration, took the sting out of death and rendered it impotent, and was able to declare: "He who believes in me will live, even though he dies."

It is the Christian faith alone that faces death bluntly, physically, and victoriously. Jesus Christ transforms it from an enemy bent upon your destruction into a friend that promises to usher you into eternal glory. Death is the consequence of humanity's sin. It is encountered and overcome by the incarnation of God through Jesus Christ who became flesh, walked among God's human creatures, died on the cross, and rose again victorious over sin, Satan, and death. You are not only a physical animal; you bear the image of God and are even now in the process of "becoming" what God intends you to be. Death is as much a part of that process as is the life you now enjoy and sometimes endure—a necessary event in the total process of God's creation.

Believe it—and rejoice, for this is the truth!

Prayer for the Day

My God, my Guide, my Master,
and my Companion,
   you have stayed close beside me through
   summers of joy and winters of discontent,
   through springtimes of promise
   and autumns of depression.
You have never left my side!
When I have fallen, you have picked me up.
When I recklessly walked the edge of ruin,
   you were there to hold me back.
Even when I screamed in protest and rebelled,
   your chastisement was gentle
   and your love was constant.
Now it is getting late, O God,
   and sometimes I feel resentful.
Forgive me for looking back, dear Lord,
   except to glory in your presence and your care
   throughout those perilous years.
I seek not to be younger in years.
   but to be young and ever vital in spirit.
Grant, my God, that your eternal Spirit
   may replenish the dry wells of my life,
   that even though my bones may ache
   and my activities diminish,
   my life may be a spring of living water
   to my sisters and brothers about me.
And forbid, O Lord, that I should ever find
   the final day of this long journey
   a day to fear or to regret.

30————Grace for Your Journey

1 Corinthians 1:3-9 "Grace and peace to you from God our Father and the Lord Jesus Christ" (v. 3).

This grace of God enables you to be and to do what he requires of you. By grace you were received into God's family through Christ's redeeming love. By grace you are made to be guiltless and will be sustained today and kept to and beyond the end of this world. Because of God's grace you are gifted and enriched with the provision and power you need to carry out God's plans for you in this life within this world. Paul writes that "you do not lack any spiritual gift as you eagerly wait for our Lord Jesus Christ to be revealed" (1 Cor. 1:7).

This is truly amazing, astounding—almost unbelievable! Yet it is true. You do not need to bemoan your inadequacies nor envy those around you who appear to be better endowed than you are. You are redeemed, forgiven, ordained for service in God's kingdom, and empowered by grace to carry out your assignment as God's child and servant.

This means that you are ready to act on your assignment to utilize God's gracious gifts for the benefit of others. Renew your commitment to God and his purposes and yield your body and being to God's grace and control. God is faithful; walk the journey of faith as a responsible servant of God within his eternal kingdom.

Prayer for the Day

Sometimes the world looks ominous to me,
O Lord,
    and I don't feel that I have what it takes
    to live as you would have me to live amid the
    pains and problems of your people around me.
I am afraid, Lord, and I look to you.
Grant me courage, O God.
You do not require that I win every battle.
You simply ask that I pick up my arms—
    or my cross—
    and enter into the arena of life.
You do not expect that I fret or fuss over the
    insurmountable circumstances that confront me.
You simply ask that I be myself—
    your child, your disciple, your representative—
    reaching out to others in love,
    helping to bear another's burdens,
    allowing your Spirit to work out
    your will through me.
So I go forth, my great God,
    by your orders, and in your power.
Your will be done, O Lord, in me and through me.

31 ———————High Hopes

James 5:1-10 "Be patient, then, brothers, until the Lord's coming" (v. 7).

It is not surprising that, while you may not be overcome with fear, you are often uneasy, frustrated, even angry about the atrocious things that happen in the world about you. Almost every newscast violates your sensibilities until you cry out for divine intervention in this planet's sad state of affairs. The world is by all appearances well on its way to self-annihilation, and the children of God appear to be helpless and incapable of arresting its mad rush to destruction.

Neither James nor any other of the apostles held any high hopes for the world as such. Their hope and their faith were in the promises and purposes of God as revealed to them through Jesus Christ. God will eventually intervene; the Lord will come, they insisted. "Be patient," James wrote, "and stand firm, because the Lord's coming is near." His message is as contemporary and pertinent as the evening news: take courage, be strong, shore up your heart, the coming of the Lord is at hand!

You will not likely accomplish anything for God by fretting about this world's condition or praying for Christ's immediate return. It is vitally important that you recognize the Christ who came at Christmas, who died on Good Friday and arose from the dead on Easter, who sent his Spirit at Pentecost, and who is even now indwelling your life. Knowing this, dedicate anew your life to carrying out your Lord's objectives which will eventually resolve in his grand intervention at the end of time.

Prayer for the Day

*I*t is difficult, my loving God, to demonstrate my
joy and reflect your love
in a world that seems to be falling apart.
Hatred and violence, dishonesty and disorder,
immorality and lawlessness run rampant
in this beautiful world you have created.
Hopelessness and despair haunt the hearts of many
men and women.
While frightened people scurry about for a place
to hide or concoct foolish gods which they think
will sustain them,
I continue to turn to you.
You are my Lord and my God.
I believe that you are present in this world
even at times when you seem so far away.
Forgive me for my impatience as I seek clear
signs of that presence.
Help me to know that you really are here and
are working out your purposes through me today.
Strengthen and sustain my faith, O God,
that I may walk my journey in joy.

32———Stop Fussing–
Keep Trusting

ebrews 11:1-8 "Abraham . . . went, even though he did not know where he was going" (v. 8).

There are days when you have to deal with a difficult person or make an important decision or confront the possibility of a serious change in your life and affairs. At these moments you have little idea of where you are going or what you should do once you get there. If anyone enjoins you to "have faith" or "trust in God," this simply doesn't appear to be very appropriate. "Faith is being sure of what [you] hope for and certain of what [you] do not see," and you are not sure or certain of anything as you face the next few hours or days in your life.

This is what the journey of faith is all about; it is facing each day of the year or mile of the journey "even though [you] do not know where [you] are going." God does not tell his children what he is going to do with their lives—or where this day's journey will take them; God only reveals to them who *he* is. This was enough for Abraham, and he obediently "went, even though he did not know where he was going."

You know how ungracious it would be to interrogate God about your future in those hours when you are nearest to God and he seems so close to you. Extend those hours to include this day and every day of your life, for God is always this close to you and will continually be with you wherever this day's journey will take you.

Prayer
for the Day

My loving God, you have been
   my gracious Leader on this long journey.
You turn my gripes into gratitude,
   my screams of despair into proclamations of joy.
You cancel out my past failures.
You love me even in my weaknesses.
You assure me of life everlasting in
   that glorious dimension that crowns the
   conclusion of my earthly pilgrimage.
Rather than fussing about my future,
   I ought to explode with praises and spend
   this life and the next in giving thanks to you.
I can do no less, Lord,
   than to live each day of the journey to the full,
   entrusting myself totally to your mercy,
   and demonstrating my joy in loving relationships
   with your children all around me.
You are my hope and salvation.
I commit the remainder of my pilgrimage
   into your hands, O Lord.
Let me be a daily reflection of your
   love and glory.

33————You Are Not Alone

John 14:15-21 "You know him, for he lives with you and will be in you" (v. 17).

The most profound and helpful message the church of Jesus is privileged to proclaim is that you are not alone. This was the promise of Christ to his disciples when he spoke these amazing words: "[He] will be in you." The presence of God throughout Old Testament times and even during the ministry of Christ was God's presence *with* men and women. From Pentecost and afterward, it was to be a presence *in* men and women. This is a spiritual mystery and it is not possible to explain or adequately articulate spiritual mysteries.

Likewise it is impossible to explain how the sunshine enters into the midst of the flower and manifests itself in all the living beauties and tints of the blossom, or how the water saturates the ground and comes forth again in the leaf and the fruit, or how the music of Handel or Bach can draw men and women of many generations into the presence of God, or how the influence and personality of a bosom friend or loved one can become a part of one's very being.

"He will be in you"; he *is* in you. It was for this that man and woman were created, and for which God had striven with his creatures throughout the ages. If it were not for Pentecost and the granting of God's Spirit to the redeemed children of God, God's purposes and the ministry of his Son, Jesus Christ, would not have been accomplished. Now God, through the Spirit, is in you. It means that whatever darkness or bleakness may overtake you on your journey of faith, you are not alone.

Prayer for the Day

O God, sometimes I am frightened
by the uncertainties and insecurities about me.
I am sorely tempted to run for my life,
to take refuge in some foolish escapade
that dims the vision or drugs the soul.
But you are my place of refuge, O Lord.
You are here; I am not alone.
You are aware of my fears and apprehensions.
You can transform my fears into a faith
that will recognize your presence,
draw me closer to you,
and enable me to shed my feelings of loneliness
in focusing upon your purposes for my life.
I thank you, God, because you are here in my world.
Even among the difficult circumstances
that plague my life,
I know I can find eternal security in you.

34——Stop the World–I Want to Get Off

Mark 1:14-20 " 'Come, follow me,' Jesus said" (v. 17).

"I want to get off," is the response of despairing and depressed people to the tragic, complex, violent events in their world. The storm warnings are out and people, frustrated and fearful, are running for their lives in search of security or some measure of serenity that will blot out this world's disturbing threats to their well-being. Those who are older tend to reach back into the past and try to hang on to forms and traditions. There are those who crawl farther back into the womb of the church and cling desperately to the "horns of the altar" as a sanctuary from life's vicious storms. There are others who latch on to those movements that feature religious ecstasy, the get-ready-for-heaven gospel, or the Christ-is-coming-soon emphasis, in response to the convulsions of this world today.

Jesus' message is not always comfortable, but this is still his message to you in this hour: "Come, follow me, and I will make you fishers of men." He does not give this earth's human creatures permission to get off this calamitous ball of clay. He invites and commands them to follow him, to serve him and fellow creatures on this world, knowing well the possible consequences of obedience to him.

The strange and wondrous thing is that it is in such obedience, which results in a loving commitment to people, that you discover an out-of-this-world joy and serenity that cannot be eradicated by those tragic, complex, violent events that are exploding all about you.

Prayer for the Day

I *live*, my God, in a churning, conflict-ridden,
revolutionary world.
It is frightening at times,
and my reaction is to retreat to the sanctuary
of the past where I assume I can be free
from the everyday tensions of this life.
I even look to my church where I hear those great
words about my safety and security in you.
Forbid, O God, that I run away from such
crises and conflicts.
You have placed me in the midst of such
and have commissioned me to serve you in
just such times as these.
Help me, undergirded with your grace,
to be filled with your Spirit and
to find my place and fulfill my responsibilities
as your child and servant.
Grant to me the courage to put my reputation, job,
income, even my life on the line
toward the accomplishment of your purposes.
May I be faithful to you in precisely
this kind of world.

35 ———————— Life-style
for Christians

Matthew 5:1-12 "Blessed are those who hunger and thirst for righteousness" (v. 6).

Mahatma Gandhi praised these words. Nietsche cursed them. Many people sentimentalize over them. Most people just bow politely to these beautiful thoughts and respectfully put them into cold storage. But always the words leap to life again to provoke and disturb. They should, for this is the Sermon on the Mount, a collection of Jesus' most profound and best-remembered words.

For non-Christians this sermon is a frustrating, impossible sort of thing. For the Christian it is something quite different. It is obvious that this sermon is not something attained or accomplished, but a life-style to reach for, aim at, focus upon. The words do not lead to salvation—except to drive a person to the need of God's grace. They are something, however, which by that grace ought to increasingly be consequential to authentic Christianity. The sermon could be a sort of portrait of a saint and result in the kind of life that will communicate God's healing and power to the lives of sick, lonely, oppressed, broken people in community and world.

For you, however, the Sermon on the Mount might be an agenda or a guide in respect to your daily activities. It will not win nor earn you God's favor; that has already been bestowed upon all who open their lives to the crucified and resurrected Christ. As a life-style it should apply to all who belong to the family of God—and one that you are empowered and expected to grow into as a redeemed and adopted member of that family.

Prayer for the Day

*D*ear Lord, many of your pronouncements
and proclamations
that were remembered
and passed on by your disciples
are difficult to understand and virtually impossible
to carry out.
They just don't fit and I can hardly
see how they apply to my generation.
They are utterly unreasonable, impractical,
and very frustrating to those who love
your words and make some attempt to live by them.
I, too, love them
but have sorely failed to embrace or
live out the kind of life-style they decree.
It is thus that they drive me to your throne of
grace and there to confess my inability
to live by your rules and instructions.
I continue to want to be what you want me to be,
to be Christ-like,
to live and love and reflect your life
and spirit amongst my peers.
My endeavors and hopes, however, fall flat;
and I so miserably relate you to my comrades.
Grant, O God, the grace and strength that is essential
in order to live out your commission and serve
as your disciple in my home, my place of work,
and wherever I am.

36————Lest You Be Disqualified

1 Corinthians 9:24-27 "So that after I have preached to others, I myself will not be disqualified" (v. 27).

You are a child of God. You are justified by faith in Jesus Christ as your Savior and Lord. It is important, however, that you keep the faith. The failures of your life are and will be forgiven, but the failure to rise from defeat and persist in your walk of faith may prevent you from experiencing the joy that could be yours.

This means that you must give priority to the business of being a Christian and that you make whatever sacrifices necessary to keep that first and foremost in your life. "I do not run like a man running aimlessly. . . . I beat my body and make it my slave so that after I have preached to others, I myself will not be disqualified."

There is a reward for those who keep the faith. It is not some sentimental, harp-playing, cloud-hopping, pearly-gate nonsense. It is eternal reality—and the answer and fulfillment to your deepest needs and longings. This will be the eternal result, not of continual success, but of staying close to Jesus Christ and being faithful and persistent in the midst of your daily conflicts.

You need not be disqualified. You abide within divine grace. As you claim God's grace and devote yourself to obedient servanthood, you will run the race successfully and will be assured of the ultimate prize.

Prayer for the Day

I dare to come before you, my great and gracious God,
> not because of anything worthy or desirable
> within me, but because of your gift of righteousness
> which you granted to me through your Son,
> Jesus Christ.

Even though I fear at times that you might give
> up on me because of my failure to truly trust and
> obey you, I know that I am not disqualified.

You are my Savior and Lord;
> I am your child and servant.

Forgive me for my feeble struggle and compromising
> tendencies, and grant to me the grace to bring my
> wayward nature under your total control.

I truly want to serve you and to emulate
> you among my fellow beings;
> I can do so only by your enabling love and grace.

Continue, my God, to hold me fast when I foolishly
> and restlessly struggle to go on my own, and to
> relentlessly pursue me if I ever leave the
> circle of your loving care.

You are my God;
> I can find no joy or peace in any other.

37 ——————How about a Mystery?

1 Corinthians 15:51-58 "Listen, I tell you a mystery: We will not all sleep, but we will all be changed" (v. 51).

In a moment, in the twinkling of an eye, at the last trumpet? And at the sound of the trumpet the dead will be raised imperishable? It's incredible! To most people utterly unbelievable! This was, however, Paul's conviction, and continues to be a conviction that energizes and motivates Christ's disciples today.

Of course it's a mystery, and it is very foolish to worry about when and where and how all this is to transpire. Paul was content and grateful in knowing that the victory through Jesus Christ *was* assured, "that death has been swallowed up in victory."

So be awake and aware—always! Even as you rest in what God has done on your behalf, be on the tiptoe of expectancy. Continue working, giving, loving, keeping the faith, and demonstrating that faith to the world of men and women about you. The time will come soon enough when all of God's children will experience together the eternal wonders of the next dimension. As for now, you, with them, need to hold on to one another in love, serve God and one another in both your vocations and avocations, and dedicate yourself in loving service to God and humanity. Be assured "that your labor in the Lord is not in vain."

Prayer for the Day

I know, O God, that this world is not my home.
It is rather more like a journey,
traveling on, always reaching for that hope
made possible through Jesus Christ who overcame
the trauma of dying and death to reign forever
over your kingdom.
I have a living hope through the resurrection of
Jesus Christ from the dead and "an inheritance
that can never perish, spoil or fade."
I am absolutely certain of this despite the
foolish doubts that annoy and frustrate me
along this journey of faith.
May this blessed assurance enable me to risk
my possessions, gifts, even life itself,
to carry out your purposes and communicate your
love to those who cross my path.
Grant, O God, that I be faithful to you
and that I, like Paul, be content and grateful
in knowing that the victory through Christ
has been assured,
that "death has [already] been swallowed up
in victory."

38 ———————— Valley
to Vision

*M*atthew 17:1-16 "Peter said to Jesus, 'Lord, it is good for us to be here' " (v. 4).

Twelve men left their jobs, homes, and families to follow Jesus. Maybe they deluded themselves into believing that he was Israel's future king and that their sacrifices would result in eventual positions of wealth and prestige as his associates. It wasn't working out that way; Jesus was no closer to earthly power and glory than when he was baptized in the Jordan River. They were in need of a vision, and in view of the trials-by-fire they would experience in future months and years, three of the disciples were permitted such a vision.

You, also, will occasionally have more than enough of valley living and will need a mountaintop experience, something that will put a glow into the daily struggle, renew the meaning and purpose of your continual battle with life, cast a bit of a halo around your perpetual conflicts. And there are occasions when that very thing will happen to you. There will be oases along your desert path that refresh and revitalize your weary spirit. They may come in the form of a Bach chorale, a Beethoven symphony, a good book, a walk in the woods or on the beach, a conversation with a dear friend, a Bible class or worship service, or a meeting with a stranger who turns out to be an angel unawares.

Then it's back to the valley again, the hours of pain and frustration, your trials and defeats, your friend's suffering. Through it all, however, there is joy—deep, profound, inexplicable—the joy of knowing that you are God's child and servant forever.

Prayer for the Day

O God, I am sometimes tired of the hard road,
the dusty valley.
My hands are dirty—my feet sore;
my heart is heavy with the concern of others.
There are those days when I desperately want
something for myself, dear Lord,
a few accolades of appreciation,
a medal or certificate of merit,
or even a commendatory slap on the back.
Give me some measure of success, O God,
some sense or feeling of being significant,
some out-of-this-world experience to give
wings to my flagging spirit.
Forgive me, gracious Father, for such unworthy
thoughts.
May the crucible and cross-bearing of this life
purge me of my lust for self-esteem.
Grant me the strength to cling tenaciously
to the joy and the assurance of your love
in the valleys through which my faith journey
will take me.

39————Temptation

Hebrews 2:14-18 "Because he himself suffered when he was tempted, he is able to help those who are being tempted" (v. 18).

Temptation! For many on Main Street it's a brand name for a seductive perfume. For the shallow and the playful it's a mischievous game. For the talented and daring it's an invitation to win another medal. For the prosperous or well-to-do it's a challenge to accumulate more. For the down-and-out loser it's the prelude to still another defeat. For the aspiring Christian temptation might be a chance to try a forbidden pleasure but it might also take the form of the "little" things: temptations to belittle someone, to ignore people's needs, or to watch television instead of finding more constructive activities.

All too often temptation takes the shape of bread that promises to satiate one's hunger, or water to slake one's thirst. Often it promises fulfillment, escape, and happiness or pokes into one's dark hours with beckoning fingers of hope and light. It may interrupt a drudge-laden routine with tantalizing excitement, or even relieve one's pain with experiences of pleasure and delight.

Temptation never lets up—and you are precariously exposed. You discover that you cannot win all the battles with temptation. Such battles may be necessary for Christian maturity. You may grow stronger in conflict, discovering your weaknesses to be channels of divine power and sustenance. God does not send temptation and will not likely intervene or come between you and your temptations. But God promises the grace to resist them. You need to claim that grace.

Prayer
for the Day

Dear Lord, I am tired and depressed.
Trying to follow you is more difficult
    than I expected it to be.
The thrill and excitement that followed my commitment
    to you and your purposes has dimmed somewhat.
Sometimes I miss the things I left behind.
I want so many things for myself, O God.
I have trouble putting the needs of others
    before my own.
There are some people who really upset me and
    I don't even want to try to love them.
I want to feel better about myself than I do,
    and to get some respect and attention from
    others around me.
I guess I'm tempted to give up and simply
    do what comes naturally.
I sometimes think I was happier back there when
    I did not take you and your life and call
    so seriously.
You know, O God, that there are siren calls
    I cannot in my own strength resist.
Grant to me the grace to be faithful to you
    and to your will for my life.

40——You Are Accepted

*R*omans 5:1-11 "We have peace with God through our Lord Jesus Christ" (v. 1).

The truth of the matter is—and this in spite of foolish efforts to placate God by means of rules and laws and traditions and customs—that you *have been* accepted by God through Jesus Christ. This is where you now stand; this is what you ought to be celebrating. This is no vain hope; it is the gospel truth. God's love and Spirit *do* abide within you.

It is when you accept and cling to what God has done for you through Christ, despite your human feelings and frailties, that the very conflicts which beset you and may even threaten to destroy you become God's tools to grind and polish and temper your spirit and prepare you for loving and obedient service.

Let this day be filled with praises! You *are* reconciled to God; you are God's forever! Now you can lend yourself to good works on God's behalf and begin to reflect and transmit to others something of your joy as God's child and the saving grace of a loving God that is extended to all who will accept Jesus Christ as the Savior and Lord of their lives.

Prayer for the Day

O God, now I know who I am.
You gave me my identity in the moment
    of my Baptism.
You touched me with your cleansing power
    and filled my heart with your Spirit.
I am accepted as your child forever.
I truly am your child,
    fallible and often very foolish.
When I stumble in my childish attempts
    to follow you,
    you pick me up and dry my tears and heal
    my wounds and draw me into your loving embrace.
I am your servant.
I am to serve you in serving my brothers
    and sisters about me.
I do not always know my future course,
    but I know where I am now.
Through the pressure of circumstances
    or the persuasion of your loving control,
    I am here to serve the people around me,
    to retain and further comprehend my identity
    by using and even in losing my life
    on behalf of others.
I am accepted as your disciple and servant.
I thank you God
    for making me valid and significant as your
    very own child and servant forever.

41————The Crucible
of Conflict

saiah 43:1-3 "When you pass through the waters, I will be with you; and when you pass through the rivers, they will not sweep over you. . . . For I am the Lord, your God" (vv. 2, 3a).

You are the victim of conflicts—some of them are fierce and long-lasting; others are subtle and soon pass. This is the law of all nature. Life is transmitted through struggle and travail; in such manner a mother gives birth to a child. Conflict is a normal part of a child's development. From the day of breast-weaning through the child's struggles in school to learn and compete and relate, conflict is always present.

This conflict is apparent in the moral and spiritual nature of God's human creatures. Where there is conflict, there is the possibility of defeat. The tragedy is not in an occasional defeat; it is in giving up the struggle, the refusal to face up to one's conflicts.

Conflict is necessary in the lives of God's servants. It purges and prepares them for productive service, and helps them feel compassion for others. So it is on the battlefield of life that you too can minister to the wounded and fallen. God reaches out to suffering humanity through those who have gone through the crucible and have experienced some of humanity's conflicts.

God may not calm the forces and gales that beat around you, but he can calm whatever storm might rage in your heart, and give you peace. God is with you as you pass through the cascading rivers and rocky paths of your earth-bound life. God is with you in the midst of your conflicts.

Prayer for the Day

O Lord, there are some people who recklessly
leap into the furnace of conflict.
They appear to have no fear whatsoever of the
uncertainties or insecurities of life about them.
They look upon life, past, present, and future,
as a challenge and appear to relinquish the past,
enjoy the present, and are looking joyfully
to the future—
and all this while I shy away from the fiery
furnace or take circuitous routes
to avoid competition or conflict.
You know my defeats, O God.
You know how incapable I am of
fighting my battles alone.
Grant to me the courage to face the crucible
of conflict when I am called to do so,
and the grace to endure,
mature, and to manifest loving concern
for my brothers and sisters as we celebrate
our journey through life together.

42 ———————— The Past Is Past

Isaiah 43:16-21 "Forget the former things, do not dwell on the past" (v. 18).

When the days darken and times in which you live become unstable, even unbearable, you probably are tempted to look back to those years or episodes in your life when you assume that you were happy or more content. Or maybe you are still burdened by some failure or sin in your past that continues to rattle its bones or inhibit you in respect to your daily activities or your outlook on the future.

The prophet was singing a song of hope and comfort to his people out of his inspired glimpse of God's plan for the future. The vision of what God was about to do would far surpass or overcome the joys or the tragedies of the past. Isaiah's message to his people may well be God's message to you at the end of a difficult day. "Forget the former things. . . . See, I am doing a new thing!" Do not totally forget all those negative episodes of the past lest you repeat them. Remember those positive gifts and blessings of the past that will encourage you to boldly face your uncertain and uncharted future.

Your hope in God continues to spell out and reiterate the fact that God still reigns and that he loves you and is working out his plan for your life in this world. This great hope also assures you that you need not be perpetually crippled or hampered by past errors or events. A new day, month, or year lies ahead of you; God will, if your hope is truly in him, continue to do "a new thing" in and through you.

A Prayer for the Day

lmighty and Eternal God,
there are some things in my past which
I cannot forget:
those times when I tried to run away from you,
or took refuge in some dead-end street
or blind alley;
those times when I took things into my own hands
and ended up hurting those I wanted to help;
those days when I was seduced by compliments
and commendations and tried to ascend to
a higher throne in my little kingdom,
or those pathetic times when I yielded to
self-pity and bemoaned my foolish
troubles and mistakes.
To believe that you can actually forgive and forget
such fractures and frailties in my make-up
is at times very difficult.
Yet I will believe it,
especially because of your gift of righteousness
that covers up my sins and self-centeredness
and begins to do "a new thing" within me.
I continue to claim your forgiveness, O Lord,
and pray that you will make even out of the ashes
of my errors something that will further
your purposes in and through me.

43————————Keep on Believing

1 Corinthians 15:1-11 "By this gospel you are saved, if you hold firmly to the word" (v. 2).

The high point, the constantly recurring theme, and the grand climax in the great symphony of the gospel is the resurrection of Jesus Christ. He died for our sins, and he arose from the dead victorious over sin and death. If this is subtracted from his message of love and hope, there is nothing left to say. You must be sure of this—his resurrection—and you can be. It was witnessed by many before you. It has or can be experienced within you.

"If you hold firmly to the word," said Paul. Equally important to your salvation in Christ is the necessity of holding fast, of keeping the faith, the determination, in spite of the plusses and minuses in your life, to keep on believing and rejoicing in the Easter event. This does not eradicate the probability of nagging doubts from time to time. You must repeatedly return to the resurrection event, the empty tomb, and to the renewal of your convictions. You will need to expose yourself to and grapple with the consequences of the resurrection of Christ in the lives of his followers throughout the centuries, and embrace anew the power and grace of that glorious happening for your life.

Keep on believing! Continue often to prostrate yourself at the foot of the cross in confession of sins, and look just as often into the empty tomb to be reassured that Jesus lives and is ever present to enable you to "hold firmly" to the faith.

Prayer
for the Day

My gracious Lord,
I thank you because my salvation is not
   dependent upon the tenacity of my professions
   or the strength of my convictions.
Nor do my strenuous efforts to please you have
   any effect upon your gifts and promises to me.
Your eternal love for me,
   your precious gifts to me,
   are not granted because of my faltering
   attempts to serve you.
They are mine because you have made me your child
   and commissioned me as your servant,
   and assured me that I shall be yours forever.
And yet, O Lord, I need your grace
   to keep on believing,
   to hold firmly to the glorious gospel
   of my salvation,
   and to dedicate daily my life to
   thanksgivings and praises even as I serve you
   in the process of serving your children
   about me.

44———If You Really Believed

Luke 24:1-11 "But they did not believe the women, because their words seemed to them like nonsense" (v. 11).

You say that you believe that Christ has been raised from the dead. You confess your faith in the living lord every time you attend your church or pray in his name. What would happen in your life, what significant changes might there be in your life, if you really believed?

If you really believed that Christ arose from the dead, you would fling aside your garments of self-righteousness, the camouflage and window-dressing of your life and fall on your face before the living Christ in confession of your sins and doubts, and in thankfulness and praise.

If you really believed in the resurrected Christ, no problems, difficulties, weaknesses or sin, no insufficiency or inadequacy could destroy you. You would discover that the power which raised Christ from the grave cannot be baffled by your thwarting frailties—that the God who performed this amazing feat of might and glory could certainly handle your pains and problems.

If you really believed in the living Christ, you would realize anew your identity and validity as God's child and servant, take up the cross assigned to you, and dedicate your gifts and energies to the splendid task of proclaiming and demonstrating that Christ is alive and that his saving grace and abundant life are available to every human creature.

If you really believed . . .

Prayer for the Day

You are alive, O Christ, and you are for real!
   You have overcome death once and for all.
   You have demonstrated your great power
   in rising from the grave.
How foolish I have been in doubting such power
   in the midst of my small problems
   and many frailties!
Now I know once more that nothing that may confound
   or perplex me is too great for you.
I pray, O God, that the power that
   raised Christ from the dead
   may raise me out of my fears and failures
   to share in that great resurrection
   and to celebrate forever
   your victory over sin and death.
May I now go forth to reflect and to demonstrate
   your resurrection power to others in this world.
Touch others through me, O God, with that power,
   that they may be raised from the dead
   to live and serve and praise you forever.

45——To This You Were Called

1 Peter 2:19-25 "Christ suffered for you, leaving you an example, that you should follow in his steps" (v. 21).

Peter undoubtedly remembered Jesus' words spoken to his disciples a few months before his crucifixion—words to the effect that those who follow him must deny themselves and carry crosses of their own. Now, several years later, Peter understood the meaning of those words.

It is doubtful that Peter would go along with much of the positive-thinking, ecstasy-seeking jargon that attracts and hooks multitudes of Christ-followers today. Suffering was an integral part of Christian discipleship in Peter's day. He prepared his converts to Christ for it and sought to support them within it. This is no less true today. Most Christians will escape the kind of violence that befell so many of those first-century Christians, but there are few who will escape suffering.

"By his wounds you have been healed." Perhaps by your wounds others about you may discover healing and wholeness. While you are not about to seek out or cause suffering if it is in your power to evade it, you need to be aware that your suffering, the crosses you bear or share on behalf of others, are to be expected and willingly embraced. They may even be necessary for your life and growth as a disciple of Christ.

"To this you were called."

Prayer for the Day

O God, I have assumed I could enjoy all the benefits
    of your grace and still revel irresponsibly
    in all the good fortune—
    health, talents, possessions—
    that have come my way.
I have cheapened your eternal love and grace
    by selfishly accepting your love and reaching
    for your promises for my benefit alone.
I now understand that I was not called to this
    and am beginning to understand what it means
    to belong to you,
    to be your possession, your child and servant.
I am supposed to be freed from the
    absolute necessity for bodily security
    or comfort—free to suffer, even to die,
    on behalf of others
    so I can tell them and reveal to them
    something of your liberating love.
But I can't do this—and won't be able to
    do this in my own strength.
I have little inclination to live for
    or to love others as you love me
    and have commanded me to love—
    unless, O Lord, your Spirit can change me from
    a sponge greedily sopping up
    all I can get from you into a fruit-bearing
    branch that exists to serve others.
Enable me, my Savior and Master,
    to take up my cross and follow you.

46—God's Grace Amid Life's Storms

Mark 4:35-41 "Why are you so afraid? Do you still have no faith?" (v. 40).

World population is exploding. The economy is on a rampage. Our environment is endangered through carelessness and waste. Our national resources are being depleted. Crime is on the increase. Hundreds of millions in this world are starving. Drought, earthquakes, and human-caused calamities are wracking our planet. Maybe you feel at times something like what these disciples felt as "a furious squall came up, and the waves broke over the boat," and "the disciples woke [Jesus] and said to him, 'Teacher, don't you care if we drown?' "

Perhaps Jesus is saying to you what he in essence said to his disciples: "Why are you such a coward? How little faith you have! I have created, redeemed, and appointed you for just such times as these. Trust me; I won't let you down. There's a quiet harbor somewhere at the end of your journey, but for now you are to abide in me and work for me in the midst of the storm."

What this gospel portion is saying is that God truly does care about you; in the midst of your insufficiency, God's grace is sufficient. This is not something you must earn, merit, or work for; it is *grace,* his great gift of love. While he may seldom cancel out the storms of your life the way he subdued that storm on the Sea of Galilee, he does promise to be with you as you face and endure and ride out the storms that swirl about you. You need only, in faith, to recognize and accept his promises and power and lay claim to his peace even in the midst of the raging tempests that beset you.

Prayer for the Day

I have gone through a painful experience, O God,
   and I sometimes wonder if you really care.
But you let it happen, Lord,
   and I keep asking *why?*
Yet the skies remain cold and gray with
   merciless silence;
   and I wonder if you really do exist.
The fact that I commune with you today
   indicates an inborn conviction that you do exist,
   and that you even know about the storm that
   assailed my life.
O God, the vacuum, the agony, the bitterness,
   and pain flattens me with despair,
   and I pray that you will fill the vacuum,
   end the agony, resolve the bitterness,
   and help me to endure the pain.
Help me, O God, to feel your loving presence
   and to lay hold of that grace which you
   have assured me is sufficient to keep
   me steady and faithful whatever the storms
   that ravage my small craft.
Do it now, Lord; please do it now.

47————Christians
Who Turn Away

Galatians 1:3-10 "I am astonished that you are so quickly deserting the one who called you . . . " (v. 6).

It is astonishing, and disconcerting, that so many people turn away from the gospel as Jesus proclaimed it to chase after some subjective ecstasy or go traipsing after a sign or miracle or vision or fall prey to some half-truth that promises to make their lives more comfortable or secure or exciting. False prophets twist the Scriptures to say what they want them to say. They enclose God with their own shallow concepts and pass this sometimes poisonous concoction to their avid followers. Paul had no kind thoughts about such individuals: "Let [them] be eternally condemned," he said.

While you may not be inclined to judge so harshly promoters of such a religion, you need to avoid them and to make certain that the gospel you accept is the gospel of Jesus Christ and not the pathetic preachments of foolish and dangerous self-styled prophets.

All Christians are tempted at times to interpret the gospel in ways that fit their assumed needs or that appear to be most reasonable. Perhaps Christians need to be shaken up from time to time to make sure that their reach for eternal truth far exceeds the grasp of human understanding, and to continue resisting attempts to package or bottle-up God in a closed system of select rules, regulations, or rituals that can be handled without too much discomfort or pain.

Let God, as revealed through Jesus Christ, be God. He is the One who loves, accepts, and commissions you for service.

Prayer for the Day

There is, O God, no way to be reconciled to you
   except through your Son, Jesus Christ,
   and the cross that he bore on my behalf.
When I gaze on that cross,
   I see in its terrible pain the joy and
   peace of forgiven sin and the freedom to live in
   loving relationships with others around me.
I discover, as well, that I too am sometimes
   destined for pain,
   that there are crosses for me to bear
   in my journey through life.
For this I have been redeemed and commissioned.
Because of this hard road along which you
   lead me, you grant me strength to endure,
   joy in the midst of suffering,
   and the guarantee of final victory.
I thank you, my loving God,
   that you who brought the promise of life
   to all people through the cross of Christ,
   will turn the small crosses of my life
   into instruments
   of redemption and channels of love to those
   I may touch on my pilgrimage through this world.

48————————Hold On

*R*evelation 22:12-21   "Yes, I am coming soon" (v. 20).

This was the message John was sending to his persecuted, imprisoned, suffering brothers and sisters in the faith: Hold on—Jesus is coming soon! Whatever else John's Revelation said to his readers—and there may have been much they understood but which still remains a mystery to Christians today—this is a message of hope and comfort to those who are trying to hold on to their faith and to their lives in that violent world of their time.

Almost every generation, in times when things become unstable and the world appears about to go out of orbit, produces its prophets that herald something of the same message: Hang in there; Jesus is coming soon! The crowds they attract give some indication of how much the message is needed, of how fears and anxieties harass people today.

Some prophets prophesy too much. They twist John's Revelation into saying or meaning something never intended by the writer. The "Jesus is coming soon" message ought to be proclaimed to every generation, but it needs to be ungarnished, freed from the tantalizing frills and thrills offered by popularity-seeking prophets and their overworked imaginations. Jesus is coming soon; that is all you need to know. There will be an end to violence, and nuclear warheads, and devastating diseases—all that is evil and ugly. There will be healing and joy, peace and rest, for those who "hold on" in faith—or allow God to hold on to them—and walk in obedience with the invisible Christ who stays with them all the way, and assures them that he "is coming soon."

Prayer for the Day

*Y*ou never said it would be easy, Lord, my
   sojourn in this uncertain, pain-ridden world.
   It wasn't easy for you.
You stood firm against Satan's temptations to win
   over the masses with cheap tricks
   and transcendent powers.
You wept bitterly over the death of a dear friend.
You were depressed by the hardness of heart and the
   rebelliousness of those who
   crowded about you.
You faced daily and dealt patiently with your
   feeble, fickle, slow-learning disciples.
You did not resist the actions of the religious
   leaders and their plans to destroy you.
Nor is it easy for me, Lord, this journey of faith
   I traverse daily in my determination to follow you.
Sometimes I think you expect too much of me.
I simply cannot measure up to your high standards.
Thus I am frightened by the evil forces that contend
   with me, depressed by my many defeats in trying
   to carry out your purposes, dismayed over the
   obstacles that impede my walk of faith.
There are days when I long intensely for your
   return to this planet,
   for the consummation of your purposes and the
   revelation of your kingdom, and for my total
   deliverance from the problems of this world.
Come quickly, my Lord,
   and while I wait, grant me the grace to hold on.

49 ————————— Do Not Lose Heart

Corinthians 4:13-18 "So we fix our eyes not on what is seen, but on what is unseen" (v. 18).

Speaking of God's light shining in our hearts Paul wrote, "We have this treasure in jars of clay." And while every jar has its flaws, God has chosen to deliver his eternal gifts to this world through such vessels. He may have to break and remake you from time to time, but use you he will—with your cooperation and obedience. He only requires that you gratefully submit your body and being for his use and consecrate your efforts and energies to his purposes.

Of course you will have problems. There will be times when you will be clobbered by conflict, even flattened in despair. There may be, real or imagined, executioners about seeking to nail you to some cross. It is quite possible that you may have to sacrifice status, popularity, even old friends, if you dare to let God have his way with you. Whatever you lose, however, you will regain a thousandfold in this life or in the next. This is the promise of your God. God does not short-change anyone.

The truth is, you don't have to be discouraged—not for long. You can even be free from the fear of failure. Only then are you truly free to live or die—to joyfully spend and expend your life for Jesus' sake.

So "do not lose heart." Following Christ is a great and wonder-filled life.

Prayer for the Day

My great God, I am still learning how to walk
on this great journey of faith before me.
I believe that you walk beside me,
   even in my mundane, ordinary, everyday living.
I know I can worship you even as I walk the busy
   streets, or through the frantic, tension-filled
   hours of the daily grind.
There are times, however, when I need to soar—
   to see mountaintops and colorful sunsets,
   to hear majestic chorales,
   to meditate on profound philosophies,
   to look beyond dusty valleys where people
   sweat and swear and struggle and suffer.
I ask not to be removed from the valley,
   or for escape or refuge,
   I ask only that my heart and imagination
   be enriched and inspired with visions
   transcending the commonplace,
   and that you grant me the grace to translate
   such visions into words and deeds
   that will enrich my life and the lives
   of earthbound men and women about me.
Help me, O Lord, to fix my eyes and the desires
   of my heart "not on what is seen, but on
   what is unseen."
Grant, O God, that I may never lose heart.

50————Really Alive

Colossians 3:1-11 "Set your hearts on things above" (v. 1).

Do you understand that you are a child of God, that God loves you and chooses that you be his child? Now you are really alive! As Christ was raised from the dead, so you have been brought from death to life and you shall live forever. You ought daily to set your heart and mind on this fantastic truth. Faith means that you begin to live and act on this truth, that this really happened, whether you feel it or not.

There are, however, some things still within you that must not be permitted to control your thinking or activities. They are those things that can come between you and God and are capable of causing harm to the people around you. Still rising out of the darkness to haunt and tempt the children of God are the shadows of lust and greed and hostility and deceit. They are like booby traps; they can destroy you and anyone close to you. You must, by God's grace and power at work within you, blast these insidious demons out of your life, and you must do it again and again, for they die hard, these agents of death.

As you grow in faith, allowing the Spirit of God to captivate and subordinate every aspect of your life under his purging love, you learn how to plug up the loopholes in your life by allowing God to flood your heart with his life. Then you will commit yourself to exercising that inflowing and outgoing love by reaching out to others in concern and compassion.

It's a great life; get on with it!

Prayer for the Day

I was surprised by joy today, O Lord.
It was a burning-bush experience,
    a Mount-of-Transfiguration episode in my life.
You were so real, so precious, so close to me.
I can't help but wish I could always feel this way.
Yet I know I must leave this mountaintop
    to run your errands and serve your children
    in the valley.
Help me to understand and really believe,
    dear Lord, that while my sense of your nearness
    may dim or diminish,
    the fact of your presence is forever secure.
You are always near;
    you are with me and will go before me
    even amidst the tragedies and dark crises
    that clutter my course through life.
Thank you, O Lord, for surprising me with joy.
May it enable me to really be alive,
    to lead to a deeper dedication to your purposes,
    and bring love and joy to others who cross my path.

51——When Your Faith Is Genuine

James 2:14-26   "Faith without deeds is dead" (v. 26).

This verse from the Bible may appear to be a small matter, but it translates into a gigantic flaw in the lives of scores of Christians. They dare to call themselves believers in and followers of Jesus Christ, and yet they act like outright bigots in their relationships with people. There are Christians who talk limitlessly about loving humanity, but are really very selective about whom they accept as the objects of their love and concern.

Christians are to love their neighbors as themselves. When their actions toward others are determined by the color of their skin, the cut of their clothes, or the size of their bank account, they are not acting like the children and servants of God. The fact is they might well be endangering their relationships to God if they neglect to give equal respect and value to all of his children around them. They need to reexamine their concepts of morality, blast out some of those silly notions that apparently influence their responses to life and people, and learn how to be loving and compassionate.

The Christian faith is not something to be exercised primarily through the rituals of a worship service. It is possible to be all mouth in terms of confessions and testimonials while the rest of the body may be paralyzed by unbelief and disobedience. It is time to tear away the fictitious labels and have the courage to confront the painful truth that you cannot talk faith unless you have faith, and if you have the faith that Jesus proclaimed and manifested, you will in turn live it and demonstrate it in sacrificial love for the human family about you.

Prayer for the Day

I claim to believe in you, O God,
    and yet I have learned or exercised so little
    in respect to my relationships with others.
I sometimes wonder whether my faith is truly genuine.
Help me to understand that faith is not simply
    a leisurely abiding in what you have done for me,
    but is also a striving and sometimes a struggle
    to lay hold of the gifts you offer.
Help me to relate in love to others.
I need help, gracious God, just to hold on to
    the faith amidst the troubles that clutter
    up my life.
I need even a greater measure of your help to
    transmit your love through my love and concern
    for your human creatures about me.
Forbid that I pin my faith on what I may feel;
    yet I pray for some sense of your presence in
    this hour that I may sing your praises
    and worship you with joy and manifest your
    love for all your creatures.
Turn up your fire within me, O God,
    that my life might glow again
    and the lives of others may be warmed through me.
I believe, O Lord; help me in my unbelief.

52——What a Savior You Have!

Hebrews 2:5-9 "We see Jesus . . . now crowned with glory and honor" (v. 9).

God, through Jesus Christ, came to his human creatures assuming a status and a position that was inferior to the very angels that were his subordinates—becoming mortal, born of a human mother, dying at the hands of his own creatures, all in order that these human creatures might live forever as his sons and daughters. And he now continues to dwell with those creatures through his Spirit who inhabits their lives, reveals his purposes, and provides his grace for joyful and meaningful living and serving.

What a Savior you have! You are no longer a stranger to God, alien to his love and holiness, a traitor to his purposes. Jesus actually became, in spiritual terms, your Brother. He participated in this humanity in order that you might become God's child. He identifies with your sufferings, shares in your weaknesses, and calls you his brother or sister.

It is an incomprehensible truth; you can become, with Christ, God's child, by identifying with this Christ and his revelations of the Father. Through Christ you now have the same Father; with Christ you become God's beloved child. It happens the very moment you by faith claim and lay hold of and submit to what God through Christ has done and continues to do on your behalf.

What a Savior you have!

Prayer for the Day

O *Jesus*, you are full of wonder and splendor!
I see the reflections of your beauty
    and hear the sounds of your majesty wherever
    I turn.
When I gaze into star-studded skies and attempt
    to comprehend the vast distances,
    I contemplate in utter amazement
    my Creator's concern for me.
I am dumbfounded that you should care about me.
And yet you have made me in your own image.
You have called me your brother and redeemed
    and reconciled me to your heavenly Father.
You have ordained me as your priest
    and chosen me to be your disciple.
You have assigned to me the fantastic responsibility
    of carrying on your creative activity.
What a Savior you are, my Lord!
How full of wonder and splendor you are!

53—You Are Equipped

2 Peter 1:3-11 "His divine power has given us everything we need . . ." (v. 3).

You are assigned to live in the end-times. You cannot run and hide as the world crumbles about you; you can stand tall and be counted. This is because you are equipped for this very thing. You simply need to acknowledge and learn how to use your equipment. Peter wrote to people who had suffered much and who expected to suffer more in the world they encountered. Now it is your world—along with everybody else that inhabits it. This world is your responsibility in these end-times that are upon you. You are to expect suffering; you are also expected to serve in the midst of suffering. For this you are equipped, as stated in Hebrews, "with everything good for doing his will."

It is natural that you question your capabilities in respect to your assignment in these end-times. In a world of computers and space shuttles and laser beams, of atheistic ideologies and totalitarian political philosophies, a world that could be destroyed in a matter of hours by a push-button war or gradually become extinct through the continual misuse and abuse of its natural resources, your first inclination may well be to burrow into some deep, dark hole and close it in after you. Your natural faculties simply do not enable you to face this kind of world. Nevertheless, you are credentialed, appointed, and commissioned for just such a time as this. And you are equipped. "His divine power has given [you] everything [you] need. . . ." Accept it, lay claim to it, and allow it to work in and through your life.

Prayer for the Day

O God, you took your Son from our midst
only to return to us by way of your
invisible Spirit.
Enable me, though I cannot see you
and even when I cannot feel your presence
to know that you dwell within me
and are here with me as I commune with you.
May your Holy Spirit so abide in my heart
and guide my activities,
that I will continue to walk in your path
and accomplish those things
you would have me to do.
Thank you, Lord, for coming to me,
for the gift of your Spirit,
for redeeming me and commissioning me
to be your child and your servant,
your vessel and vehicle in extending your
kingdom in this world about me.

54————A Time to Celebrate

Revelation 7:9-17 "Praise and glory and wisdom and thanks and honor and power and strength be to our God for ever and ever" (v. 12).

This is not a time for despair; it is a time for celebration! The resurrected Christ is with you. He is present with you amid the trials and tribulations of your tempestuous world. He is about to reappear and to gather together his faithful followers into the fully revealed and eternally reigning kingdom of God. This great, long-awaited event is about to take place, and the suffering, celebrating children of God of all nations and generations are invited. Christ will once and for all reveal himself as the living, conquering, victorious Lord of heaven and earth. Evil will be eradicated, all stumbling blocks will be removed; those who oppose God and his people will be overcome; the spiritual forces of evil will be bound and destroyed.

Sorrow will turn to joy, night into day. Tears will give way to joyous laughter; ugliness will yield to beauty. "Every knee shall bow . . . every tongue confess that Jesus Christ is Lord." On this great day the suffering martyrs, the struggling saints, the priests and prophets, the servants and disciples of all ages will be united together to sing their praises to their eternal Savior and King.

Words cannot describe it—this incredible event about to take place, but Jesus is coming soon to take his church to himself.

Let your celebration begin even now!

Prayer for the Day

You are here, O God; you are now!
It is indeed time for celebration!
Your promises have been proclaimed
throughout the ages.
With voice and musical instruments,
with lovely melodies and joyful sounds,
your name has been heralded
and your great deeds and words celebrated.
Now it is my turn to worship you,
to announce your presence and loving concern
for the inhabitants of this world.
Help me, O Lord, to fill my life, my home,
my times of work and recreation,
even the streets and marketplaces,
with the glad, joyful sounds of celebration.

55—Meaning in Misery

Psalm 138 "Though I walk in the midst of trouble, you preserve my life . . . with your right hand you save me" (v. 7).

The most destructive type of suffering is pain without purpose, misery without meaning. One's suffering becomes critical not so much in the physical hurt it inflicts as in the person's inability to discover any logical reason for it. The Christian faith offers such meaning and purpose. It asserts that though God does not intend one's suffering, he involves himself in it. He has done this through Christ who suffered on your behalf and is truly able to "sympathize with [your] weaknesses."

It is his presence in your trials and conflicts today that gives meaning and purpose to them. "In this world you will have trouble," said Jesus (John 16:33b). "But take heart! I have overcome the world." He who turned the defeat of the cross into the victory of the empty tomb has made available his power to work similar miracles in your life. Your misery, be it physical pain or personal anguish, is not the end of life. It may well be a new beginning.

No one is immune to suffering. Nor does God offer to shelter his children from such as long as they are upon this planet. When you commit yourself into the hands of your loving God, you will find the grace to endure suffering gracefully—and it will then assume some meaning and purpose, and may even become the basis for self-renewal and great compassion for others.

Prayer for the Day

F ather in heaven,
I never expected that the journey of faith
would be a flower-strewn path through
this life, but I hoped that there would be
more sunny days than I have known.
Nor do I believe that my troubles and misfortunes
are in some measure indicative of my small faith
or my shallow commitment to you
and your purposes for my life.
Yet I long so much for more sunshine along my course.
I simply cannot feel your presence
when I have trouble-fraught days.
There is no one else to turn to.
I am discomfited, anxious, lonely, and sometimes
afraid in hours of darkness.
O God, may your Word speak to me,
and your promises reassure me,
your Spirit work some miracle within me,
that I may remain faithful to you in
times of distress.
And may you somehow use even those hours and days
of unhappiness to carry out your purposes
in and through me.
I am grateful, dear Lord, that you accept me as I am,
and are able to use me as your servant,
and will abide with me whatever may be the
troubles I cause or confront in the hours
and days ahead of me.

56—Go and Wash Feet

ohn 13:6-17 "Now that I, your Lord and Teacher, have washed your feet, you also should wash one another's feet" (v. 14).

During the last meal Jesus had with his disciples, the very eve of his betrayal and crucifixion, he knelt to "wash his disciples' feet, drying them with the towel that was wrapped around him." It was an incredible act in the eyes of the disciples—and even incomprehensible—at least until after he was resurrected and reappeared as the living Christ to ordain and empower them to continue his ministry in the world about them.

What Jesus may be saying to them—and to you—through this remarkable incident is: "This is what it means to carry on my work and to obey my Father's command to love your fellow beings as yourself. It means not simply your condescending willingness but your eagerness to stoop to the humblest act of service on their behalf. This is what I have done in descending from heaven to stoop to your needs, in shedding the glory and power of divinity to become identified with your humanity. Now this is the measure in which you are to carry on my ministry: to meet your fellow beings in loving concern and utter humility at the point of their greatest and most immediate need."

You are born to be a servant. If you are to truly serve Christ, it may well involve washing another's feet, engaging in a most humble and apparently unspiritual act of loving service to the person closest to you or the neighbor next door.

Prayer for the Day

I confess, O Lord, that it is not easy
to be all things to people about me,
that I have no inclination whatsoever to serve
others whatever their needs may be.
I can sometimes testify about your love
or even tell them about your saving grace.
I am quite discerning about what is wrong
in their relationship to God.
Your example and call to feed the
hungry or visit those in prison or help others
with their burdens seem less important than the
need to convert them through the preaching of
the gospel.
And yet I see your concern and compassion
for those to whom you spoke and those you helped
and healed in your ministry on this planet.
Help me, my Lord, to realize how much you have
done for me, the significance of your compassion
and concern in my life,
that I may overcome my self-centeredness with love
and compassion for those about me.
Teach me, Lord, how to wash feet,
how to love others as they are,
and to do for them what is needed—even those
unspiritual things that appear
to be so unimportant to me.

57———Maybe Your God Is Too Small

John 6:35-59 "Unless you eat the flesh of the Son of Man and drink his blood, you have no life in you" (v. 53).

After the feeding-the-5000 miracle, the multitudes, impressed with such a remarkable activity, pressed in upon Jesus. They came not to worship him, but to speculate about him: "What a king he would make! He could supply all our needs and wants!" This kind of Christ they would gladly follow. So Jesus immediately set about to undermine such ridiculous concepts concerning himself and attempted to point up their true need—the need of restoration and reconciliation to God.

You understand far more about Christ's person and purposes than did this speculating crowd, but it may be that your God is still too small. Have you accepted only as much of him that serves your selfish purposes or conforms to your formulas and schemes?

To simply embrace the message of his forgiving love and his promise of eternal life may not be enough. Perhaps you still need to learn the meaning of eating his flesh and drinking his blood. To "eat" and "drink" Christ dramatizes your need of becoming identified with him, of making him an integral part of your being, of uniting totally with him and his purposes. It means, as well, that you who eat of the Bread of Life are to become nourishing bread to the lives of people about you. Only when you receive Christ as he is, in all that he is, as he declares himself to be, can God become large enough within you to do something for you and through you.

Prayer for the Day

I am sorry, O God, that while I am finding joy
and contentment in my relationship to you, I am
also seeing the need to become aware of my faults.
I am beginning to realize how much I have
abused your love and compassion for me
by using you as my servant
rather than following you as my Lord.
I have made you into a small god,
a spiritual concoction that is anything but the
true God in my life.
Forgive me, gracious and ever-loving Father,
for trying to use you even as I try to use
others to shore up my ego or pacify my
anxious and insecure heart.
Lead me into the intimate, risk-filled depths of an
authentic relationship with you so that you may
truly be God in me and through me.
Enable me to identify with you as the Bread of Life
and the Living Water, and to become a witness to
your grace to others around me.
I must continue to claim your forgiving love and
promise of eternal life,
and I want very much to continue feeling
secure in you.
May that security resolve into my becoming an integral
part of your being, totally identified with you
and your purposes, even to the point of being
nourishing bread and refreshing water in the lives
of your children with whom I come in contact.

58 ——— The Blessing
of Struggle

omans 5:1-5 "We also rejoice in our sufferings, because we know that suffering produces perse-
verance" (v. 3).

Blessed are those who struggle, for they shall become strong; this is not one of the Beatitudes, but it
could have been. This was certainly the sincere conviction of the apostle Paul. Indeed, the person who has no
conflict in life would be the one to be pitied. He or she
must be living a cocoon-type existence, immersed in
false comfort or fat-bellied contentment. He or she
would not be likely to make much of a contribution to
the welfare of humanity.

Despite those people for whom sainthood appears
to come so easily, whose halos sit firmly on their heads
even when the world is falling apart about them, you
are likely to continue to struggle. And where there is
conflict and struggle, there is bound to be a measure of
failure. This element of failure, however, has been fore-
seen and accounted for by the redeeming love of God
through Jesus Christ. Thus, failing is not as much a tragedy as is ceasing to struggle.

Whatever form the enemy of your soul may assume,
you must continue to do battle with it. When you fail,
and you will at times, you can claim God's forgiveness
and power, and rise to fight once more. If you remain
sensitive to divine leading and receptive to divine enablement, you will by divine grace become stronger
through your struggles and strivings and will ultimately
be victorious.

Prayer for the Day

I have honestly tried to serve you, Lord,
   to love my neighbor,
      to share myself and my possessions with others.
But it seems that wherever I go,
   I run into stone walls and thorny bushes.
Some of the people I reach out to help turn against me.
Is it really true, O Lord,
   that I am expected to be like you?
Yet it is this to which you have called me.
For this you have redeemed and commissioned me.
Because of your love for me and
   your claim that I am your child,
      you grant me the strength to endure,
      joy in the midst of struggle and crisis,
      and the assurance of ultimate victory.
Pull me out of my sorrow and self-pity;
   I claim your help because
   I am your child and servant.
Teach me, O Lord, how to accept and cope with struggle,
   how to accept my status as your beloved
   child and servant,
      how to accept the validity and power that
      go with it,
      and to walk and serve in joy.

59———God Does Care

1 *Peter 5:6-11* "Cast all your anxiety on him because he cares for you" (v. 7).

"No man cares for me," agonized the psalmist on one of the blue-Mondays of his life. The statement is supposedly attributed to David and was spoken while he was hiding from King Saul in a dark cave. There are, no doubt, caves along your sojourn through life. You probably duck into one of them now and then to hide from something that frightens or threatens—and there you moan out your loneliness and despair, telling yourself lies about God's indifference and your fellow beings' unconcern about your problem.

You may have good reason for doubting other peoples' concern for you; they are often too preoccupied with their own failures or successes to coddle you in your confusion and confoundment. Over and above the fallibilities of human beings, however, is the eternal truth of God's love and concern for you. "What is man that you are mindful of him, the son of man that you care for him?" queried the psalmist (Psalm 8:4). He answered his own question: "You made him a little lower than the heavenly beings and crowned him with glory and honor." Jesus said, "I know my sheep, and my sheep know me . . . and I lay down my life for the sheep" (John 10:14-15).

The children of God can emerge from their caves of loneliness and self-pity and reach over and around the apparent lack of human concern into the very heart of God.

God cares for them; God cares for you.

Prayer
for the Day

Merciful God,
today must be one of those days when my
self-esteem is at an all-time low.
Compliments are hard to come by,
and any reviews in respect to my activities
or accomplishments would probably
be negative.
My self-worth is in question,
and I seriously wonder why I should venture
forth to take on my little world when I
feel I have so little to contribute.
I don't feel needed or loved in this hour.
Forgive me, Lord, for wallowing in self-pity;
but I need to hear again the promise that you
will always be with me,
"even to the very end of the age,"
that you are walking this journey of faith
with me as my Brother and my Lord.
Your words of comfort and challenge through
the prophets and apostles and the uncountable
saints that have gone before me,
the gift and presence of your Spirit within me—
these will sustain me.
You do care for me;
I am continually the object of your concern.
Draw me into the activity of this day, Lord,
with renewed faith and the conviction that I
am your child and servant forever.

60 ──────────Reasons
for Rejoicing

uke 10:17-24 "Do not rejoice that the spirits submit to you, but rejoice that your names are written in heaven" (v. 20).

You have good reasons for rejoicing today. You can walk and work, study or play—and rejoice—because your significance in God's eyes is not dependent upon the feeling or the fact of success. Your joy as the child and servant of God is not to be measured by your accomplishments or achievements. You are significant apart from success if you are related to God through faith in Christ and you are walking in relationship with him.

How can you know that your name is "written in heaven"? You know that you are a forgiven and accepted child of God. "There is no condemnation for those who are in Christ Jesus," wrote Paul. Truly, this is your primary reason for rejoicing.

This means, of course, that you bring your sins and wrong-doings to God and that you hear and accept the glorious message and gift of salvation—that Jesus Christ has already suffered the consequences of guilt on your behalf. Also this means that you persistently and perpetually entrust your life wholly and totally to God and that you accept Jesus Christ and his gracious pronouncements and promises.

Times of ecstasy may be few and far between, but the joy of God's acceptance of you and his love for you shall be forever.

Prayer for the Day

I do praise you, O God.
As long as I have breath in my body,
    I will praise you.
You created the world and all that is in it.
You can heal the wounds and mend the fractures of
    this disjointed planet.
You tenderly reach out to the oppressed and
    reveal your concern for the lost and lonely.
You watch over your own and you love them
    and care for them.
You are my hope and salvation,
    my morning sun and evening star,
    my shade in the desert heat,
    my warmth in the cold of the night.
You are the Bread of Life, and a life-giving spring
    when my soul is parched and hungers for righ-
    teousness.
You are the ultimate fulfillment of my deepest longings.
There is reason for rejoicing,
    and so I praise you and rejoice in you.
I am yours, O Lord, yours forever.
Grant that my life be a perpetual offering of praise.